Judy

I am so grateful for your guidance and support for my little chapter. Page 20 does not do your effort justice but is proof of my appreciation

Paul

Reflections on Diversity in the Massachusetts Legal Profession

Past and Present

Edited by
The Honorable Rudolph Kass

Susan M. Finegan
Joyce Kauffman
Renée M. Landers
Jennifer Mather McCarthy
Paul J. McNamara
John Ward

MCLE
LEGAL
HERITAGE
Series

2150191B01

Printed in the United States of America

This publication should be cited: *Reflections on Diversity in the Massachusetts Legal Profession: Past and Present* (MCLE, Inc. 2014)

Library of Congress Control Number: 2014947057
ISBN: 1-57589-860-8

Massachusetts Continuing Legal Education, Inc.

Ten Winter Place, Boston, MA 02108-4751

800-966-6253 | Fax 617-482-9498 | www.mcle.org.

Foreword

Reflections on Diversity in the Massachusetts Legal Profession is the latest title in MCLE's growing Legal Heritage Series, established to celebrate Massachusetts' rich legal history and to support MCLE's scholarship initiatives.

This book presents a varied collection of personal narratives and historical accounts by Massachusetts lawyers of different religions, genders, races, and sexual orientations. Some pieces present a history of exclusion and bias leading to increased inclusion and acceptance. Others present personal stories. Still others reflect on how the author's background influences his or her practice today. Whether the authors' reflections are grounded in the past or the present, it is MCLE's intent that this collection provide an opportunity for the reader to reflect on the issue of diversity in the Massachusetts legal profession and that it raises even more questions for future discussion and further reflection.

Acknowledgments

First and foremost, MCLE expresses sincere thanks to this book's editor, the Honorable Rudolph Kass, for his excellent and thoughtful review of the book's contents and for contributing a chapter as well. We also express thanks to Susan M. Finegan, Esq., Joyce Kauffman, Esq., Renée M. Landers, Esq., Jennifer Mather McCarthy, Esq., Paul J. McNamara, Esq., and John Ward, Esq., for writing chapters. We thank them for accepting our rather open invitation to write and reflect on a topic that has many possibilities and by its nature cannot possibly cover everything worthwhile. This publication would not have been possible without their extensive time and efforts.

We also extend special thanks to Charles Riordan of Boston College Law School for his research assistance with Chapter I; to Professor Virginia G. Drachman, Rebecca Rogers, Esq., and Sarah Wald, Esq., for allowing us to adapt their materials from another MCLE Legal Heritage publication, *Breaking Barriers: The Unfinished Story of Women Lawyers and Judges in Massachusetts*, for Chapter IV; to the Honorable Dermot Meagher for providing us with his essay on becoming a judge for inclusion in Chapter V; and to Gary Buseck, Esq., for his feedback on Chapter V.

Additionally, we would also like to acknowledge the work of MCLE publications and production staff in putting together this publication.

On behalf of Jack Reilly, Publisher, Maryanne G. Jensen, Editor-in-Chief, and the MCLE Board of Trustees, our appreciation extends to all whose talent and hard work helped create this book.

Alexis J. LeBlanc
Publications Attorney
October 2014

About the Editor

HON. RUDOLPH KASS is a retired associate justice of the Massachusetts Appeals Court. Currently, he is associated with the Mediation Group in Brookline. Justice Kass is a graduate of Harvard College and Harvard Law School.

About the Authors

SUSAN M. FINEGAN is a litigation partner in the Boston office of Mintz, Levin, Cohn, Ferris, Glovsky and Popeo, PC, where she serves as chair of the Pro Bono Committee and chair of the Hiring Committee. Previously, she was legal director of the Victim Rights Law Center. Ms. Finegan is a graduate of Dartmouth College and Boston College Law School.

JOYCE KAUFFMAN is a principal of Kauffman Crozier LLP in Cambridge, where she focuses on family law, with an emphasis on issues impacting the LGBT community. She is a member of the National Family Law Advisory Council of the National Center for Lesbian Rights and the board of directors of Gay & Lesbian Advocates & Defenders (GLAD). Ms. Kauffman is a graduate of the University of Massachusetts at Amherst, Lesley University, and Northeastern University School of Law.

RENÉE M. LANDERS is a professor of law and director of the health law concentration at Suffolk University Law School in Boston. She is a former president of the Boston Bar Association, the first woman of color and the first law professor to serve in that role. Professor Landers is a graduate of Radcliffe College and Boston College Law School.

JENNIFER MATHER McCARTHY is an associate in the Boston office of Mintz, Levin, Cohn, Ferris, Glovsky and Popeo, PC, where she focuses her practice on litigation. She regularly takes on cases through the firm's domestic violence program, providing pro bono legal assistance to low-income victims of domestic violence. Ms. McCarthy received her B.A., M.A., and J.D. from Boston College.

PAUL J. McNAMARA is a partner at Looney & Grossman LLP in Boston, where he specializes in property and probate law. He is the current president of the Catholic Lawyers' Guild of the Archdiocese of Boston and the immediate past president of the 275-year-old Charitable Irish Society of Boston. Mr. McNamara received his B.A. and J.D. from Boston College.

JOHN WARD is the founder of Gay & Lesbian Advocates & Defenders (GLAD) in Boston. The first openly gay male lawyer to practice in Boston, he has dedicated his legal career to fighting for protection for LGBT and HIV-positive individuals. He is a graduate of Fordham University and Boston University School of Law. Mr. Ward currently resides in San Francisco with his husband, Alain Balseiro.

Table of Contents

I

The Experience of Catholic Lawyers *1*

Paul J. McNamara, Esq.

Introduction 1

How Catholic Lawyers Are Perceived by Others 3

Reflections on the Purpose for Establishing Boston College Law
School 4

The Elements of a Faith Relied on in the Practice of a Catholic
Lawyer... 10

Faith Based Opportunities During the Course of Legal Practice 16

Tensions 17

Conclusion: The Francis Effect 18

II

The Experience of Jewish Lawyers *25*

Hon. Rudolph Kass

III

The Experience of African-American Lawyers *35*

Renée M. Landers, Esq.

Introduction 37

Massachusetts as an Early Leader in Opportunities
for Black Lawyers 38

Blacks Slowly Gain Leadership in the Judiciary and Public
Life in the Second Half of the Twentieth Century 43

Twentieth Anniversary of the Equal Justice Report 46

Black Lawyers in Private Practice and Corporate Law Offices 47

Blacks in Academia 49

The Role of Black Lawyers in Bar Associations 50

Surveying the Past and Scanning the Horizon 51

IV

The Experience of Women Lawyers 59

Susan M. Finegan, Esq.
Jennifer Mather McCarthy, Esq.

Introduction 59

The First Women Lawyers in Massachusetts 60

Portia Law School 66

"The Golden Age of Opportunity" 67

Discrimination 69

The First Women Judges 72

Conclusion 75

Biographies of Selected Pioneering Massachusetts Women Lawyers
    Anna Christy Fall 75
    Emma Fall Schofield 76
    Elizabeth Marston 77
    Sadie Lipner Shulman 78
    Inez C. Fields... 80

V

The Experience of LGBT Lawyers 85

Joyce Kauffman, Esq.
John Ward, Esq.

The Early Years: Survival and Beyond 85

Individual Lawyers' Experiences
    Hon. Dermot Meagher 93
    Sara G. Schnorr 109
    Hon. Maureen H. Monks 113
    Hon. Paula M. Carey 117
    Mary L. Bonauto 119
    Robert L. Quinan 127
    Hon. Angela M. Ordoñez 131
    M. Barusch 135

CHAPTER

I

The Experience of Catholic Lawyers

Paul J. McNamara, Esq.

Introduction

In explaining the integration of one's faith into the practice of law, one first must ask what we, and all faith-based practitioners, actually mean by faith. For a Catholic, it means in its simplest form that belief in God as He is revealed in Jesus Christ, doing good as opposed to evil, and the search for truth, are absolutes and the very foundation of faith. For a Catholic these absolutes are formulated through the prism of the teachings of the Roman Catholic Church and Scripture, including both the Old and New Testaments.

So how does one incorporate faith into the practice of law? One doesn't. A Catholic already brings his or her faith to the practice because the person and his or her faith are inseparable. We are the sum of our parts; our upbringing, our experiences, and our religious and lay education.

The values of a Catholic lawyer are in part molded by his or her Catholic faith. A Catholic lawyer, when he or she thinks about subjective and objective situations in the law, cannot separate his or her identity from legal analysis and practice. The complexities of faith in the practice of law involve details I hope to explore in this chapter.

The integration of faith is not unique to a Catholic lawyer. Recently, I was pleased to appear as a panelist at an interfaith workshop for students at Harvard Law School. The topic of the workshop was integrating one's faith into the practice of law. The panel consisted of a Muslim, an Episcopalian, and a Mormon. (Unfortunately, the Jewish representative was kept in Washington, DC, because of the weather.) No member of the panel found any systemic institutional bias against an employee practicing his or her religion. All concentrated on the aspects of bringing the precepts of their faith to their practices. One concept that was shared by all of the panelists was that if one has not come to the practice of law with a full understanding of his or her identity and beliefs, it is harder to identify a threatened wrong or fight for principle when the occasion arrives. Alternatively, if one is grounded in faith, it is easier to live out the moral and ethical choices arising in legal practice. To be clear, an atheist may also choose a moral, ethical life in order to confront unethical conduct or immoral conduct. An atheist on the next panel at the same workshop accepted it may be easier to confront unethical or immoral behavior if properly prepared, but it is "damn hard to confront it," properly prepared or not, atheist or nonatheist.

How Catholic Lawyers Are Perceived by Others

This book's intent, in part, is to explore some of the history of bias against lawyers based on their religion, gender, race, ethnicity, or sexual orientation. In this chapter, that proposition brings us to reflect upon the impediments that affected Catholics graduating from law school in twentieth-century Massachusetts.

From colonial times to the late nineteenth century, Catholics were the targets of bigotry and discrimination. For sure, individual Catholics succeeded in their educational and business endeavors during such times. The issue for us to explore is whether, in the twentieth century, religious bigotry prevented Catholics from entering the legal profession and obtaining positions for which they were qualified.

To answer this question, I spoke with a number of attorneys who had plenty of stories of lawyers who did not receive interviews for jobs they were qualified to hold or who did not seek employment with established law firms because they felt barred. In concluding that their Catholic faith was not the primary barrier to a good position with a premier employer or law firm, I relied heavily on the recollections of lawyers with whom I spoke, particularly three lawyers who graduated from law school in the 1950s through the early 1960s: James J. McCusker, Esq., Portia Law School (now New England Law | Boston), Class of 1963, a sole practitioner in Boston; James R. DeGiacomo, Esq., Georgetown Law School, Class of 1956, currently of counsel to Murtha Cullina; and David Walsh, Boston College Law School, Class of 1953, formerly counsel to the New Haven Railroad for over forty years.

Before I met with those lawyers, I recalled a study I did during a sabbatical year at Boston College Law School. The study traced the employment history of Boston College Law School graduates from the 1930s through the late 1950s and revealed that a large number of the graduates worked for federal government agencies as diverse as the Post Office and the FBI, and for the state government (including the court system), and even attained the occasional state judgeship. Rarely in those early years did a BC Law graduate go to the well-known banks or well-known law firms.

The lack of first-tier jobs for Catholics (many were Irish, Italian, or Polish) during the 1930s, 1940s, and 1950s was evident. This was borne out in my interviews. Employment opportunities beyond government and one's ethnic group were limited or nonexistent in the 1930s, 1940s, and well into the 1950s. The question is whether these impediments were a result of anti-Catholic bigotry. To my surprise, all three interviewees agreed that anti-Catholicism did not appear to be the main obstacle to getting a job in the higher echelon of Boston employers, including law firms. The first problem was the educational institutions one graduated from, not his or her religion. Harvard Law and Yale Law graduates seemed to receive favoritism. Also, ethnic origin, and not religion, barred entry, assuming one was offered an interview at all. Although it was often hard to separate ethnicity and religion in those years, being Catholic did not specifically prevent one from getting a position; one's parentage and one's school were the main impediments. This discouraging state of affairs only loosened when the various ethnic groups began to have economic power, becoming sought-after customers for businesses and clients for law firms. The rising power of the archbishop of Boston during this time also helped. Archbishop Cushing, later Cardinal Cushing, was a formidable figure in the areas of politics, business, and education. When asked to rank the difficulties of getting an attractive position in the top tier of businesses and law firms, my interviewees ranked the right school (education) as the number one obstacle; ethnic origin as a close second, and being Catholic as third.

Reflections on the Purpose for Establishing Boston College Law School

With education being the biggest stumbling block to the right position, there was clearly a need for a preeminent Catholic law school. In 1929, the year Boston College Law School was founded, the only two

Boston-area law schools accredited by the American Bar Association and the Association of American Law Schools were Harvard Law School and Boston University Law School. Neither school enlarged its capacity to accommodate the growing population of the city and Commonwealth. Boston College graduates who did not gain admission to one of these two schools could only go to an unaccredited law school if they wished to stay in Massachusetts to pursue a law degree.

The Boston area's growing population, which increased demand for law school, was matched by a corresponding growth in Boston College's undergraduate population. Teeming with ambition and fueling its own goal of embracing all opportunities for growth allowed by its charter, Boston College decided to establish its own law school. In 1929, Boston College Law School was established in the city as part of a larger scheme to locate BC's graduate schools in a downtown Boston campus apart from its main campus in Chestnut Hill, some six miles west of the city. Boston College Law School also was a product of good economic times, providing students, with ambition and the means to pay, an opportunity for a law school education. Boston College Law School had both a day division and a night division (the only accredited night school in the city at that time).

Boston College Law School opened with a Harvard Law School flavor. Most faculty members held Harvard degrees, casebooks used were authored by Harvard professors, and the method of case study used was the instruction method fathered by Harvard Law School Dean Christopher Columbus Landell.[1] The 1939 Boston College Law School bulletin stated:

> The prime purpose of a course in law is to provide adequate preparation for the practice of law in any state, and for this reason the general principles of the common law are emphasized. As a result, the student is better qualified to enter the general practice of law than would be the case if instruction were narrowly limited to one particular jurisdiction. Comparative study is made of

> decisions in all jurisdictions where the English System of law prevails with special attention being given to Massachusetts, the other New England States, and New York State.[2]

The 1949 Boston College Law School catalog states the purpose more fully, as follows:

> The purpose of the Boston College Law School is to prepare young men and women of intelligence, industry and character, for careers of public service in the administration of justice, and to equip them for positions of leadership in advancing the ideals of justice in our democratic society. With this two-fold objective, students are given a rigorous training in the principles and rules, the standards and techniques of the law, not as positivistic ends in themselves, but as rational means, capable of constant improvement, to the attainment of objective justice in civil society.
>
> For the Boston College Law School is dedicated to the philosophy that there is in fact an objective moral order, to which human beings and human societies are bound in conscience to conform, and upon which the peace and happiness of personal, national and international life depend. The mandatory aspect of the objective moral order is called the natural law. In virtue of the natural law, fundamentally equal human beings are endowed with certain natural rights and obligations to enable them to attain, in human dignity, the divine destiny decreed by their Creator. These natural rights and obligations are inalienable precisely because they are God-given.

They are antecedent therefore, both in logic and in nature, to the formation of civil society. They are not granted by the beneficence of the state; wherefore the tyranny of a state cannot destroy them. Rather it is the high moral responsibility of civil society, through the instrumentality of its civil laws, to acknowledge their existence and to protect their exercise, to foster and facilitate their enjoyment by the wise and scientific implementation of the natural law with a practical and consonant code of civil rights and obligations. . . .

The Boston College Law School is deeply conscious of the heritage of the American philosophy of law. It is profoundly aware of its educational responsibility to the students who seek its instruction, and of its civic responsibility to the people who look to its graduates for professional service and civic leadership. Hence, it strives to impart to its students, in addition to every skill necessary for the every-day practice of law, an intellectual appreciation of the philosophy which produced and supports our democratic society. For it is only by the intellectual recognition and the skillful application of the natural law to the principles and rules, the standards and procedures of the civil law, that civil society can hope to approach the objective order of justice intended by the Creator for rational and spiritual human beings.[3]

The point is that educating the growing population was only a part of the task; the main objective was and is to provide excellent legal training designed to instruct the whole person regardless of race, creed, or color. The actual unfolding of the stated purpose from the 1930s to the 1960s and the 1980s may be a story in itself. The emphasis on excellence in the legal curriculum and a standard of excellence in the students admitted led to a question seriously debated among alumni and faculty: Is Boston College Law School a law school founded and supported by a Jesuit Catholic university, or is Boston College Law School a Jesuit Catholic law school? The debate will probably always be with us, but when Rev. William P. Leahy, S.J, president of Boston College, speaks of the law school, he is emphatic in his description of the law school as a Jesuit Catholic law school.

What is a Jesuit Catholic Law School and why is it important to the question of how the Catholic Faith is understood in the daily practice of law? Who are we?

The Catholic intellectual tradition is not a static body of knowledge; it is a conversation across time, with variant strands and a range of contested positions. People of all traditions can participate in the conversation, learning from one another and contributing in a range of different ways to the conversation. Fr. David Hollenbach S.J., late head of the Society of Jesus, suggests this sort of conversation is sustained by one of the distinctive resources of the Catholic intellectual tradition, the virtue of intellectual solidarity defined as:

"Taking other persons, societies, and cultures seriously enough to engage them in conversation and debate about what makes life worth living, including what will make for the good of the city and the globe. Such a spirit goes beyond tolerant non-interference with the beliefs and life-styles of those who are different. To be sure

> intellectual solidarity recognizes and respects
> these differences. But it differs from pure tolerance
> by seeking positive engagement with the other
> through both listening and speaking. It is rooted
> in the hope that understanding might replace in-
> comprehension and that perhaps even agreement
> could result. Where such engaged conversation
> about the good life begins and develops, a com-
> munity of freedom begins to exist."[4]

Intellectual solidarity and justice might be understood as the cardinal virtues at the heart of a Jesuit law school. Jesuits wanted to educate a certain kind of person committed to serving the common good of society with an apostolic commitment to shape students and society through education. Education from the beginning of the Society of Jesus was to "help souls" through rigorous study, the purpose of which was to form people of good character committed to the common good of society. A commitment to justice is essential to this goal.

The current Boston College Law School mission statement reflects this Jesuit goal as follows:

> Boston College and its law school are rooted in
> the Jesuit tradition of service to God and others.
> In that tradition, we believe that the purpose of
> higher education is both the search for know-
> ledge, and the preparation of women and men
> who are moved to a constructive, responsible,
> and loving use of their knowledge. The Law
> School recognizes its commitment to social and
> economic justice, and strives to advance this
> commitment both through its curricular offer-
> ings and in the extracurricular projects that it
> supports. We encourage our students to develop
> their own individual commitment to others and
> to explore those themes which are central to the

Jesuit tradition: the dignity of the human person, the advancement of the common good and compassion for the poor. We seek to train a diverse student body not merely to be good lawyers, but to be lawyers who lead good lives, and who will be prepared to seek and to find meaningful work in service to others that will enrich their communities.[5]

This mission statement, and its reference to Ignatian spirituality, are good bases for discussing what exactly the elements of faith are that Catholic lawyers have in common and employ daily.

The Elements of a Faith Relied on in the Practice of a Catholic Lawyer

At the outset of this chapter I stated that faith is an integral part of who we are as Catholic lawyers. Faith also means accepting that we are to live life as Christ wants us to live. That means working for the common good in the hope that such a life is inseparably linked to justice. Justice should also be inseparably linked to engaging other traditions in dialogue. As Catholic lawyers, we cannot live our lives apart from faith, and our faith requires us to interact with lawyers of other religious traditions. Interaction with other traditions is a part of Ignatian spirituality. It is also a part of the contemporary decrees of the Society of Jesus's thirty-fourth general congregation. Decree 5, entitled "Our Mission and Interreligious Dialogue," provides in part:

General Congregation 34 encourages all Jesuits to move beyond prejudice and bias, be it historical, cultural, social or theological, in order to cooperate wholeheartedly with all men and women of good will in promoting peace, justice, harmony, human rights and respect for all of

God's creation. This is to be done especially through dialogue with those inspired by religious commitment, or who share a sense of transcendence that opens them to universal values.

In fact, this ancient yet continuous conversation is part of the Catholic intellectual tradition that guides us ordinary lawyers as we go about our daily lives. This conversation may in many ways be helped by recalling that Ignatius teaches God is in all things and in all places. Ignatius aligns us with God working alongside us in what has been referred to as "the buzzing, demanding reality of everyday life."[6]

Father Frederick Enman, S.J., asks Catholics and non-Catholic lawyers to recognize that the origins of our Western legal system are rooted in Scripture:

- Genesis: humans are made in the image and likeness of God;

- Exodus: rescue the poor and lowly slave people; freedom;

- the Covenant: treat each other with mercy and compassion;

- the Ten Commandments: make life in community possible;

- the law codes of Exodus, Deuteronomy, and Leviticus: concern for widows, orphans, strangers, the poor; do not take bribes; and

- Isaiah 58 and Matthew 25: integrity, honesty, compassion, and especially dignity.

Examples of practical applications of the above that are evidenced in our laws and legal systems include

- property laws assuring a balance of power between tenants and landlords;

- basic elements of a valid contract: mutual assent, consideration, capacity, and legality;

- consumer protection laws;

- the U.S. Constitution and its guarantee of equal protection for all;

- our system of taxation, which attempts to address issues such as fairness and who in our society should bear the burden of the highest taxes; and

- corporate laws governing securities and ensuring protections for investors against Madoff-type schemes.[7]

Further, to understand one's faith-based practice for a Catholic is to accept that the sacrament of baptism establishes that every person is a child of Christ, to recognize that free will is bestowed on every person, and to recognize that the gift of reason is bestowed on every person. These are truths developed over time by philosophers and theologians, foundational truths embodied in faith. They are also part of the complexities of faith as experienced in the Catholic lawyer's "buzzing demanding realities of everyday life."

Professor and former Boston College Law School Dean Daniel R. Coquillette:

> Recent developments in legal education, particularly legal realism, have emphasized the function of law as an "instrument" to achieve particular political, social, and economic ends. The older ideals of a "neutral" rule of law have been debunked as, at best, a pious myth, and, at worst, a deliberate effort by the powerful to exploit the weak under an illusion of "fairness" of principle. Many students become convinced that professionalism means being willing to pursue the ends of others, irrespective of the means. It ultimately puts the client, for better or worse, in the driver's seat, and the ideal of justice becomes secondary.[8]

Others have opined that law school students may find themselves being formed to play the restricted role of skilled technician, a role disconnected from the larger questions of human aspiration.

How saddening to have one's ability to perceive and appreciate human concerns and values that underlie law and lawyering restricted by thinking of oneself solely as a skilled technician or an instrument to achieve a particular political, social, or economic end. As a person of faith, one must try to understand that one's responsibilities are in trying to rid oneself of bias when confronting the amalgamation of confusing facts presented in the course of legislating, by plaintiffs and defendants in a court of law, in understanding a private client's assignment to his or her lawyer, or for a law professor teaching the student to "think like a lawyer." These should be seen in the light of an exhilarating challenge, where all aspects of one's humanity are brought to bear on a solution or plan of action, all of which belies a description of lawyering as just a technical skill. To the contrary, as a Catholic lawyer you will recognize the dignity of each participant. If you believe every human being is made in the image and likeness of God, you cannot deny him or her the dignity he or she deserves. As Catholics we are taught to love the sinner (dignity) but hate the sin. In other words, as Catholics we do respect a flawed personhood.

Rather than cataloging the ways our faith bears on the practice of law, I prefer to call attention to an address at 2009 delivered by former dean of Boston College Law School, John Garvey. Dean Garvey chose one virtue he believed was peculiarly Catholic and fits well with the nature of our business in ways that lawyers sometimes may overlook.

> We are taught in law school to be zealous advocates on behalf of our clients. Zeal in defense of a just cause is admirable. It is the trait the general public instinctively associates with lawyers. 'I have been wronged by my business associates [my employer] [the government] [the oil company next door], and I need an advocate who

will stand up for me.' I do not mean to denigrate that service. It *is* one of the things we do.

But the law is not war. The people on the other side of our lawsuits and transactions are not the enemy—they are our brothers and sisters in Christ. There comes a time in every adversary relationship when the virtue called for is not courage or zeal but forgiveness. It may not be until recompense is made. At that point, though, we need to do what we can to heal the relationship that a wrong has disrupted. . . .

I probably don't need to add that there is room for this virtue not just in our clients' relations with their adversaries, but in our own relations with opposing counsel. This might, in fact, be the place where it is called for first of all. I have a tendency to fly off the handle when dealing with children who stay out past curfew. My wife reminds me that I'm not really teaching them what time to come home—I'm teaching them how to deal with children who stay out past curfew. They learn from what we do, not from what we say. It's not exactly the same with clients. But the snares of the legal system are, for them, a strange environment, and they learn something from our behavior.[9]

Dean Garvey's address was delivered at the 2009 Red Mass in Massachusetts. The Red Mass is an annual tradition for Catholic lawyers dating back to the Middle Ages. The mass is celebrated annually to mark the opening of the court's term. The following is a description of the Red Mass from the Catholic Lawyers' Guild of the Archdiocese of Boston.

Liturgically, the Red Mass is celebrated as the Solemn Mass of the Holy Spirit. Its name derives from the traditional red color of the vestments worn by clergy during the Mass, representing the tongues of fire symbolizing the presence of the Holy Spirit. The Judges of the High Court, who were all doctors of the law, also wore red robes or academic hoods. With so many participants in red, the celebrations became irrevocably known as the Red Mass. The Red Mass historically marked the official opening of the judicial year of the Sacred Roman Rota, the Tribunal of the Holy See.

In the United States, the Red Mass tradition was inaugurated on October 6, 1928, at old St. Andrew's Church in New York City. Since then, the Red Mass has been celebrated throughout the United States each fall before the U.S. Supreme Court's term begins.

The first Red Mass celebrated in Boston is eloquently described by Reverend Charles Donovan in his book, *The History of Boston College*:

"On October 4, 1941, the Solemn Votive Mass of the Holy Spirit, known in a tradition which goes back many centuries in Rome, Paris and London as the 'Red Mass,' was celebrated for the first time in Massachusetts to mark the opening of the judicial year. The ceremony, which took place in the Immaculate Conception Church, was under the auspices of Cardinal O'Connell and the Boston College Law School.

The function drew the most distinguished legal assemblage ever gathered in the state for a religious service. Governor Leverett Saltonstall and Mayor Maurice J. Tobin led the procession…up the center aisle. Among the participants were the chief justice and the full bench of the Massachusetts Supreme Judicial Court; the judges of the Massachusetts probate courts and The United States Courts; judges of the land courts, district courts, and the Boston municipal courts; the attorney general of the state and his entire staff; the United States attorney and his entire staff; district attorneys and assistant district attorneys; and representatives from all the law schools and law societies in the state."[10]

Needless to say, the Red Mass is not a state matter; it is not an establishment of religion. Attendance is entirely voluntary and non-Catholics are guests. It remains for many Catholic lawyers, however, an important faith-related annual tradition.

Faith Based Opportunities During the Course of Legal Practice

Moving from the noble abstractions of faith, let's look at the practical application of trying to expand faith for the common good. We have seen above John Garvey's clear view that advocacy in any form is an opportunity to bring to bear one's faith. Our relationships with clients and adversaries alike should reflect our faith's instruction that we are all God's creatures. We should contend with our brothers and sisters with that thought in mind. As I write this line I am overcome with thoughts of the church scandals of every nature. I also reflect back on good and evil, free will, reason influenced by a blunt conscience, failure of developing a good moral character packaged in us humans, religious and lay alike; not hypocrisy.

There are plenty of ways to contend with our fellow human beings in practical terms, such as social outreach to the sick, the poor, the homeless, and the incarcerated. There are many opportunities in cause-based practices, such as public defenders and advocacy groups for a large variety of issues, all designed to promote justice and the common good.

Tensions

There exists tension between Catholic teaching and government regulations and statutes. Catholic lawyers, judges, and law professors are faced with tough faith-based choices. Calling on the faith-based elements discussed above, sometimes one can only refuse and walk away. One very serious disruption I participated in as a member of the board of trustees of Catholic Charities of Boston occurred in 2006 when the organization requested an exemption from a state law requiring that all adoption agencies allow same-sex couples to adopt children. Though all agreed the agency did outstanding work, no exemption was granted by the governor or the legislature. The teachings of the church thus gave the cardinal archbishop no viable alternative but to require the adoption agency at Catholic Charities to disband in an orderly manner. The vote tore at the conscience of every board member, those in favor and those opposed to Catholic Charities' abandonment of one of its seminal missions.

I do not see my role in authoring this chapter as defending the teaching of the church, defending the actions of government, or defending the decisions of individuals involved in conflicts like the example above. It is sufficient to say the tensions are numerous, the human toll is serious, and that the application of faith to the various issues in conflict is indeed difficult. Catholic and non-Catholic lawyers have reached out to all sides to create a dialogue with those of opposing views. Catholic and non-Catholic lawyers on all sides of such issues have sacrificed not only their time and treasure but more importantly their reputations. Professional opportunities have been sacrificed, and too much time has been spent away from families. God bless these conversations that they will, in many cases, yield an understanding of conflicting views and yield to intelligent compromise.

I should add that I understand that non-Catholic lawyers face similar tensions of value systems and duty to law, statutory or case-made, and duty to clients.

Conclusion: The Francis Effect

I have been asked to include in this chapter what effect I have seen in Catholic lawyers' practice resulting from the explosion of enthusiasm and popularity of Pope Francis' interviews and writings since becoming pontiff. The truth is I have no idea, but the question opens a doorway to conclude this chapter by reflecting on Pope Francis' leadership.

I have written above of the Catholic intellectual tradition's call for dialogue and understanding when approaching the myriad of conflicting facts and perceptions in our client matters. How essential it is to rid ourselves of our biases to properly understand the problem at hand and to deal fairly with all parties involved. I believe Pope Francis is showing us the way by his words, inspiring the actions of others who see the wisdom and benefits of thinking anew and opening a broad dialogue.

Pope Francis is deemphasizing many of the negative ideas, the "thou shalt nots" of religious thought. He is thinking in new ways on old problems. An example is the abortion issue. The fight of many Catholic lawyers has been courageous and very successful. Even while the efforts of many are necessarily expended, Pope Francis says these efforts should not, even on this important issue, prevent other important aspects of Catholic teaching and social justice from being improved and promoted. Instead, we must broaden our thinking. Recently the Catholic Lawyers' Guild of Boston held a seminar on divorced and remarried Catholics who as a result are barred from receiving the sacraments. Pope Francis has called for a gathering of bishops to study this problem, among others. The Very Reverend Mark O'Connell, Guild Chaplain and Judicial Vicar of the Archdiocese of Boston, revealed there are a number of thoughtful, gentler approaches to the problem that are compatible with church teaching and traditions, which the Council of Bishops will be taking up. One area to be discussed is rethinking the manner in which an innocent spouse, who has no control over destructive behavior of his or her spouse, should be embraced by the church where an annulment is not currently available.

As Catholic lawyers we ought to be conscious of the benefit of open dialogue in our practices. I wrote earlier in this chapter of John Garvey's call for lawyers to pave the way for forgiveness at the end of a contested matter. Whether or not one agrees with John Garvey, the word "forgiveness" gives rise to warm feelings. I have been thinking recently of the word "surrender," which prompts an abhorrent visceral reaction. If a lawyer might see surrender not as an act of defeat but as a doorway to be used with dignity during the course of an extremely bitter negotiation, then he or she might better consider whether or not to pursue a course of action which makes no fundamental difference in the outcome sought. This concept is not at odds with vigorous defense of a client, follows the Catholic tradition of reason and fairness, and allows for John Garvey's call for forgiveness. This strategy follows the example of Pope Francis in ways of seeking the truth through open thinking and dialogue. The tactic of controlled surrender of certain actions is prudence, not defeat. I remember an interview with the late Cardinal O'Connor of New York at the time of his retirement, in which he was asked to name his greatest lesson from his tenure as the cardinal archbishop of New York. His answer: "don't swing at every pitch." Good advice for all of us.

Indeed, Catholic lawyers struggle to reconcile their religious beliefs with their everyday practices no more or less than non-Catholic lawyers struggle to incorporate their own values and belief systems into their legal practices. As stated at the outset of this chapter, it is anything but easy. However, we are strengthened by a tradition that supports an ordered society for the common good. Pope Francis himself urges us to recognize that in our buzzing, demanding everyday lives, there is joy.

I am pleased to acknowledge the extraordinary support in writing this chapter that I have received from the following persons: Professor Judith McMorrow, Boston College Law School; former Dean Daniel R. Coquillette, Boston College Law School; Rev. Frederick R. Enman, S.J., Boston College Law School; Rev. Gregory Kalscheur, S.J., Boston College Law School; Very Reverend Mark O'Connell, Judicial Vicar of the Archdiocese of Boston; the staff of the Boston College Law School Library; the quiet venue of the Boston Athenaeum; the partners, associates, and staff of my law firm, Looney & Grossman LLP; and Alexis J. LeBlanc and the professional staff of MCLE. I also extend thanks to Charles Riordan of Boston College Law School for his editing assistance, and to my sons, Paul J. McNamara and Bernard S. McNamara, and my friend, neighbor, and former English teacher, Suzanne M. McGowan, for serving as proofreaders and critics. Finally, special thanks to Mary H. McNamara, my loving wife and lifetime partner, for her patience and encouragement.

Timeline of Selected Notable Persons and Events

1245	The tradition of the annual Red Mass begins in France.
1780	The Massachusetts Constitution permits Catholics to publicly worship.
1801	The Supreme Judicial Court states that "Catholics are only tolerated here, and so long as their ministers behave well, we shall not disturb them. But let them expect no more than that."
1806	Murder trial of James Halligan and Dominic Daley in Northampton. Amid a fervor of anti-Catholic sentiment, the two men are found guilty of the murder of a mail carrier. They are hanged. Years later the real murderer confesses.
1906	Frank Leveroni becomes Massachusetts' first Italian Catholic judge when he is appointed a special justice of the Boston Juvenile Court.
1915	James Bernard Carroll is the first Catholic appointed to the Massachusetts Supreme Judicial Court.
1918	Attorney David I. Walsh is elected as Massachusetts' first Irish-Catholic U.S. Senator.
1929	Boston College Law School is founded.
1941	The first Red Mass is celebrated in Boston at the Immaculate Conception Church.
1943	The Justinian Law Society is founded as the Massachusetts Italian Bar Association in order to provide an opportunity for Italian-American lawyers to meet and discuss difficulties they faced in the profession at a time when many doors were closed to them. Today the society's mission is to "strive to preserve the traditions of Italian culture and to recognize the contributions of Italian-Americans to the law."[11]

1987	Catholic Lawyers' Guild of Boston is founded. The guild's "primary mission is to sponsor or facilitate spiritual, social, educational and charitable opportunities and events that celebrate the richness of [the Catholic] faith and the nobility of [the legal] profession."[12]

Endnotes

[1] *See generally* Todd F. Simon, *Boston College Law School After Fifty Years: An Informal History, 1929–1979* (Boston College Law School 1980).

[2] *Boston College Bulletin: The Law School* 17–18 (Apr. 1938).

[3] *Boston College Bulletin: The Law School* 14–15 (Apr. 1949).

[4] *See* Gregory A. Kalscheur, S.J., "Conversation in Aid of a 'Conspiracy' for Truth: A Candid Discussion About Jesuit Law Schools, Justice, and Engaging the Catholic Intellectual Tradition," 43 *Gonz. L. Rev.* 559, 566–67 (quoting David Hollenbach, S.J., Address at Loyola University Chicago: The Catholic University and the Common Good (Nov. 6, 2007)).

[5] "Mission Statement," Boston College Law School, *at* http://www.bc.edu/schools/law/prospective/history/mission.html.

[6] *See* Fr. Howard Gray, S.J., "As I See It: Ignatius's Method for Letting God Shine through Life's Realities (Boston College Center for Ignatian Spirituality), *at* http://www.bc.edu/bc_org/prs/ignsp/articles/article1.html.

[7] Interview with Fr. Frederick M. Enman, S.J., Chaplain, Boston College Law School.

[8] Daniel R. Coquilette et al., *Lawyers and Fundamental Moral Responsibility* (Lexis Nexis 2d ed. 2010).

[9] John H. Garvey, Address at Catholic Lawyers Guild of Boston Red Mass, Sept. 20, 2009, *at* http://www.mdcathcon.org/library/resources/RLLaunch/GarveyRed-Mass-2009.pdf.

[10] "About the Red Mass," Catholic Lawyers Guild of the Archdiocese of Boston, *at* http://www.clgb.org/the-red-mass/ (quoting Charles F. Donovan, et al., *History of Boston College* 188–89 (1990)).

[11] Justinian Law Society of Massachusetts, *at* http://justiniansofmass.org/about.

[12] "About CLGB," Catholic Lawyers Guild of the Archdiocese of Boston, *at* http://www.clgb.org.

II

The Experience of Jewish Lawyers

Hon. Rudolph Kass

In the beginning, there was Brandeis. His place and experience in the legal profession during the 1880s differed from his contemporaries of Jewish ethnicity. Brandeis graduated from Harvard Law School first in the Class of 1878. Together with his intellectual horsepower, he possessed youthful charm and grace.[1] Second in the class was Samuel Dennis Warren, scion of a Brahmin family.

Although a Jew from Louisville, Kentucky, Brandeis, with "unaffected suavity of his manner,"[2] blended into Boston society. In 1879, Samuel Warren and Brandeis set up practice as Warren and Brandeis in space at 60 Devonshire Street, for which they paid rent of $200 per year.[3] Brandeis took time off to clerk for Chief Justice Horace Gray of the Supreme

Judicial Court. Gray's appraisal of Brandeis was not understated. "I consider Brandeis the most ingenious and most original lawyer I have ever met, and he and his partner are among the most promising law firms we have got."[4]

In 1889, Warren left law practice to manage the family paper business. Eight years later, the firm had become Brandeis, Dunbar & Nutter. Edward F. McClennen was a younger recruit to the firm. A.T. Mason, an early biographer of Boston, wrote that Brandeis was innocent of religious observance and in his law practice and social life did not identify "with any one race, sect, or interest. His friends were indiscriminately Jews and Gentiles."[5]

His easy integration into Boston professional life and society did not, however, shield him from an undercurrent of anti-Semitism when, in 1917, President Woodrow Wilson nominated Brandeis to the Supreme Court of the United States. There had never before been a Jew on that court.

Jewish graduates from law school who did not have the spectacular brilliance and charisma of Brandeis—and nobody did—followed different and in some respects stonier paths. There was an understanding at the time of the turning of the nineteenth century to the twentieth that Jews would not be welcome in established Boston law firms. This was less "anti"—as peers Jews were well regarded—than a sense that Jews would not "fit in" to a wholly white Anglo-Saxon office.

Lee M. Friedman, like Brandeis, was the scion of a prosperous mercantile family of German-Jewish origin that had arrived in the United States in the mid-nineteenth century. Friedman was also a high achiever who moved easily in Boston's intellectual aristocracy. His Harvard College roommate, Louis C. Cornish, who became a Unitarian minister, was influential in sparking in Friedman an interest in his own religious heritage and in the history of Jews in the United States. In time, Friedman became a leader of the Jewish community in Boston and a significant collector of Judaica that he left to Harvard College.

Although his academic career at Harvard Law School, from which he received the LL.B. in 1895 with honors, was distinguished, Friedman did not knock on any doors of established law firms. He opened his own law office in Boston in 1897. Friedman had a sense of the value of "diversity" in a law office.[6] In 1903 he took in as a partner Percy A. Atherton, of WASP antecedents. The practice took the name Friedman and Atherton—such was the name's panache that the firm retains that name today.[7] Friedman earned and enjoyed a high-altitude reputation at the bar. A man of great energy, Friedman was known daily to walk to work in downtown Boston from his home in Brookline.

Three years after Friedman opened shop, Edward S. Goulston established the firm Goulston & Storrs. Goulston, again, was of German-Jewish heritage. His father was a well-established tobacco merchant, his mother a pianist. The elder Goulstons saw to it that their children were well educated and pushed in the direction of the learned professions. Edward Goulston first worked in retail by day and attended law school by night. Upon his graduation, he could launch his practice with a ready client base in the garment industry, notably the Leopold Morse Company. In the next generation, a Leopold Morse Goulston turns up as a member of the firm. Herbert B. Ehrmann, who, like Brandeis, hailed from Louisville, Kentucky, became a partner of Goulston & Storrs in 1921. He was an associate defense counsel, with William G. Thompson, in the appeal of Sacco and Vanzetti from their conviction of murder in the Superior Court. Ehrmann's career flourished, not only as a lawyer but as a leading figure in Jewish organizational life on a national and international scale. At a time when established, largely white Anglo-Saxon Protestants seldom hired Jewish law school graduates, Ehrmann felt a moral compulsion to hire Jews as associates. As we shall see, in the late 1960s, and more dramatically in the 1970s, that exclusivity gave way to meritocracy and consequent diversity in what had been Jewish, WASP, or Catholic law firms.

During the 1880s and 1890s, virulent anti-Semitism and lethal pogroms in the Russian Empire stimulated a wave of Jewish immigration to the United States for refuge and opportunity. The new immigrants found both, and were able to make modest livings. They were also able to educate their children in good public schools. A share of those American-born progeny gravitated to the professions, particularly law and medicine. Simultaneously, their generational contemporaries made their way in the shoe and textile business—manufacturing, wholesale, and retail—real estate, construction, vaudeville, movies, other retail sectors, and finance. There was, therefore, a client base.

Rosenfield v. United States Trust Co., 290 Mass. 210 (1935), illustrates that sort of synergy. The plaintiffs were in the retail jewelry business and had been in negotiations to rent store space at the corner of Winter and Washington Streets in Boston. The defendants were a bank (United States Trust Co.) and Abraham Ratchesky, a principal officer and stockholder of the bank. In his own right, and as trustee of a testamentary trust, Ratchesky owned that property; he was seconded in the discussions by a younger family member, Alan R. Morse. As to the terms of the lease, the parties agreed on much, but, as the Supreme Judicial Court determined, not enough: the negotiations were "imperfect" and did not support a breach of contract action. D. Stoneman and A.A. Tepper appeared for the proposed tenant; Lee Friedman and Frank Kozol appeared for the landowner. All the actors in the case, clients and lawyers, were members of a developing, upwardly mobile Jewish community.

There follow some accounts of the formation of small law firms by enterprising lawyers of Jewish background for whom prospects for entry into an established law firm ranged from unlikely to none.

In 1920, Harry N. Guterman and his brother Abraham opened shop at 19 Milk Street, Boston, as "Guterman & Guterman." During the 1920s and early 1930s, theirs was largely a commercial and insolvency practice. In 1928, Harry Guterman hired Harold Horvitz, then three years out of Harvard Law School. Their practice broadened into labor, real estate, and business law. Howard Rubin joined in 1938. In 1953, the firm name became Guterman, Horvitz & Rubin. Harold Horvitz became active in the Massachusetts Bar Association, whose members elected him president in 1960–62.[8] In 1968, Stanley Rudman, who had developed a lively business litigation practice, joined Guterman, Horvitz & Rubin, and it became Guterman, Horvitz, Rubin & Rudman. In 1984, following the emerging style of law firm names, it became Rubin and Rudman.

One firm that has resisted shortening its name is Mintz Levin Cohn Ferris Glovsky and Popeo, PC, but it has a logo that says "Mintz Levin." Its origins are in the friendship of Harriet Cohn and Charlotte Levin, who introduced their spouses, Haskell Cohn and Benjamin Levin, to each other in the 1930s.

Haskell Cohn had graduated from Harvard Law School in 1925. With a push from Dean Roscoe Pound, Cohn got a job at Hale and Dorr. Cohn did well there and became a junior partner. Also doing very well was David Burstein, a junior partner of Jewish heritage who was senior to Cohn at Hale and Dorr. In 1933, Cohn concluded he should strike out on his own in partnership with Benjamin Levin. In the depth of the Great Depression, Cohn called on his senior partner, Reginald Heber Smith, to tell him about his decision. Smith said, "You're either the biggest damn fool in the world or you're much smarter than I ever thought you were." Years later, Haskell Cohn had a photograph of Reginald Heber Smith on the wall, signed: "Haskell, we still miss you."

Herman Mintz joined laterally. He had arrived in the United States in 1892 at the age of six. The family settled in the North End. Mintz's father was a doctor; his mother was a midwife and delivered all the Jewish babies in the North End for 25 cents a birth. Those fees she would put in a box to save for the education of her two youngest sons.

Herman graduated from Harvard Law School in 1910 and, as was often the pattern then, started his own practice, not as an associate, but rooming, apprentice-like, in the office of an established lawyer—in this case Abraham K. Cohen, who was a part-time judge of the Boston Municipal Court. In return for desk space and some secretarial help, Mintz did some legal work for Judge Cohen without charging fees for it. By the time Levin and Cohn opened shop in 1933, Mintz had become a seasoned and successful solo practitioner. Levin and Cohn had an extra office in their suite and suggested that Mintz join them. For a number of years, Mintz was a tenant, but also a colleague. The arrangement matured into partnership. The firm's name—Mintz, Levin & Cohn—reflected the order of the partners' admission to the bar.[9]

Matthew Brown also had his first job at Hale and Dorr. When he asked for certain days off to observe the Jewish high holidays, he was told, "No, Matt, you have to row the boat." That made Brown think he better row his own boat.

Hirsh Freed had spent several years as an assistant corporation counsel in the City of Boston Law Department, a favored entry point for promising law school graduates during the Great Depression. He also served as a member of the state Public Utilities Commission. Freed had learning, legal technical skill, as well as political savvy that he lavished upon Boston mayoral and state gubernatorial campaigns.

Alford Rudnick had a well-tuned small business practice. They formed a partnership in the late 1940s: Brown, Rudnick and Freed. In about 1959, they joined with Henry Gesmer. The firm became Brown, Rudnick, Freed & Gesmer. Gesmer hailed from Quincy. He was one of the last great utility fielders in the practice of law. There was nothing he couldn't do and do well—be it trying a case, handling real estate transactions or corporate securities issues, organizing a bank, organizing and advising small business corporations, or advising on taxation or a motor vehicle accident.

During roughly the same period, Charles Goldman and John S. Slater went into practice as Slater and Goldman, and built an active civil practice. The firm later merged with Widett & Kruger, creditors' rights specialists, and became Widett, Slater and Goldman.

Arthur Sherin was related to the Rabb family, which founded and built Stop & Shop, a relationship that launched the firm of Sherin and Lodgen.

Looking at these law firms, it does not escape notice how significant, in the era of the 1930s, 1940s, and 1950s, Boston Latin School and Harvard College were as links between Jewish graduates of law schools and a growing client base. Another professional cross-fertilizer was activity in omnibus charities like the Combined Jewish Philanthropies and United Way.

Entry into established and establishment law firms, as the careers of Haskell Cohn and Matthew Brown illustrated, was not foreclosed, just difficult. David R. Pokross, for example, after graduating Harvard Law School, found a job at Gaston, Snow, Saltonstall and Holt, where he did good work but was fired in 1933. It was not anti-Semitism, it was the Depression. Pokross was hired by Peabody, Brown, Rowley & Storey, where he had a distinguished and long (until he was ninety-four) career. Charles E. Wyzanski, Jr., became an associate at Ropes, Gray in 1932; left to serve as solicitor to the U.S. Department of Labor; returned to Ropes in 1937; became a partner in 1938; and remained at the firm until his appointment in 1941 to the U.S. District Court for the District of Masachusetts.

World War II had a great impact. Soldiers, sailors, Marines, and air corps members who had served together developed bonds that superseded class and religious distinctions. That and the G.I. Bill of Rights were altering the social and ethnic stratification of earlier times—not only in the legal profession, but in American society overall.

An example is Edward J. Barshak, a celebrated leader of the bar in the second half of the twentieth century. The G.I. Bill made it possible for him to attend Columbia Law School. He joined as a third member of an existing two-man practice of Bert Sugarman, a trial lawyer, and Sumner Rogers, a civil business generalist. In 1959, they were joined by Steven J. Cohen and the firm became Sugarman, Barshak, Rogers and Cohen. It still flourishes under that name. It is larger, albeit boutique in a sense that it concentrates in litigation, and fields a team of lawyers of wholly varied ethnicity and gender.

In 1943, Henry E. Foley, who had been corporation counsel of the City of Boston in the mid-1930s and dean of Boston College Law School in 1938, founded, with Garrett Hoag, a law firm with an express program of meritocracy, without regard to ethnic background. The firm became Foley, Hoag & Eliot. Joining it after World War II's end was Lewis H. Weinstein, an already seasoned litigator and pioneer in the merging fields of housing and urban renewal. Other veterans who joined that firm, but only after attending and doing well at law school, were Herbert Berman, H. Kenneth Fish, Hans F. Loeser, and Jerome Preston, Jr.

By the middle of the 1960s, the class, ethnic, and religious lines that had characterized Boston law firms dissolved. Intellectual horsepower, temperament, identifiable skillsets, and character (insofar as an interviewer could assess it) trumped social origin. This reflected not only the times but the competitive sense of the law firms whose client bases were not segregated. Class consciousness became not only bad form but was bad for business.

Timeline of Selected Notable Persons and Events

1900	Goulston & Storrs is founded. In 2014, the firm ranks as the ninth largest in Massachusetts with 155 lawyers.10
1917	Louis Brandeis becomes the first Jewish person to serve on the U.S. Supreme Court when he is appointed by President Woodrow Wilson.
1930	Sadie Lipner Shulman becomes the first female Jewish judge in Massachusetts when she is appointed a special justice of the Dorchester Municipal Court.
1933	Mintz Levin Cohn Ferris Glovsky and Popeo, PC, is founded and in 2014 is ranked as the fourth largest law firm in Massachusetts with 270 lawyers.11
1942	Charles E. Wyzanski, Jr., is the first Jewish person to serve on the U.S. District Court for the District of Massachusetts.
1952	George Fingold becomes the first Jewish person elected to statewide office (Massachusetts attorney general).
1955	Joseph Schneider is elected president of the Massachusetts Bar Association. He is the first Jew to hold the position.
1961	Jacob J. Spiegel is the first Jewish person to serve on the Massachusetts Supreme Judicial Court.

Endnotes

[1] A.T. Mason, "Brandeis, A Free Man's Life," 46–47 (1946).

[2] A.T. Mason, "Brandeis, A Free Man's Life," op. cit. at 47, 61.

[3] A.T. Mason, "Brandeis, A Free Man's Life," op.cit. at 56–57.

[4] A.T. Mason, "Brandeis, A Free Man's Life," op.cit. at 61.

[5] A.T. Mason, "Brandeis, A Free Man's Life," op. cit. at 441.

[6] It is highly doubtful that in the dawn of the twentieth century the word "diversity" carried the meaning of ethinic, racial, religious, and social inclusion that it does now.

[7] Names of law firms in the second half of the century expanded and then contracted: e.g., Friedman, Atherton, Sisson & Kozol back to Friedman & Atherton; Ropes, Gray, Best, Coolidge, & Rugg back to Ropes & Gray; Brown, Rudnick, Freed, Berlack & Israel to Brown, Rudnick. But Hale & Dorr to Wilmer, Cutler, Pickering, Hale & Dorr, although is known as Wilmer, Hale.

[8] The first Jew to occupy that office had been Joseph Schneider, who served as president of the MBA from 1955–57.

[9] Concerning the history of Mintz, Levin I am indebted to a delightful oral history of Richard G. Mintz taken by Jeffrey S. Robbins in the form of a deposition.

[10] *See* "100 Largest Law Firms in Massachusetts 2014," *Massachusetts Lawyers Weekly.*

[11] *See* "100 Largest Law Firms in Massachusetts 2014," *Massachusetts Lawyers Weekly.*

The Experience of African-American Lawyers

Renée M. Landers, Esq.

"What is striking is the role legal principles have played throughout America's history in determining the condition of Negroes. They were enslaved by law, emancipated by law, disenfranchised and segregated by law; and, finally, they have begun to win equality by law. Along the way, new constitutional principles have emerged to meet the challenges of a changing society. The progress has been dramatic, and it will continue."

> —*Remarks of Thurgood Marshall, Annual Seminar of the San Francisco Patent and Trademark Law Association, Maui, Hawaii, May 6, 1987*

"The cause of the Colored man, in whatever section of our country, expressly is really my own cause: and it would be monstrous indeed if I did not so regard it."

> —*Macon Bolling Allen, First black lawyer admitted to practice in Massachusetts (1945)*

"Though the first black lawyers, men and women, endured trials and tribulations along the way, they were never deterred from their central objective—the emancipation of their people in the New England states and beyond."

> —*J. Clay Smith, Jr.,* Emancipation: The Making of the Black Lawyer, 1844–1944, *at 114 (1993).*

Introduction

When J. Clay Smith, Jr., published *Emancipation: The Making of the Black Lawyer, 1844–1944*, his authoritative examination of the history of black lawyers in the United States, in 1993, he concluded his examination of the careers of leading black lawyers in New England by observing the inextricable connection between the efforts of individual lawyers to build successful law practices or careers in public service, and the work of eliminating the legal rules and institutions that denied blacks legal equality based on race.[1] This work of building a more just system of laws and institutions helped black lawyers acquire the skills, a sense of purpose, and the professional recognition necessary to develop strong careers. To identify an alignment of the career development of lawyers with law reform efforts to improve the status of the community of blacks and African Americans is not to suggest, however, that in 2014 African-American lawyers do not still lag white lawyers in achieving law firm partnerships, judgeships, and other key indicia of career achievement. The gains in formal legal equality for the black community have not removed all the barriers to career achievement for black lawyers, just as blacks continue to suffer discrimination in the larger society. So emerges another theme characterizing the experiences of black lawyers—that despite gains, the gains are fragile and black lawyers remain underrepresented in many roles in the legal profession.

To understand the experience of blacks and African Americans who have been and are lawyers in Massachusetts requires an examination of the history of participation in the legal profession and an assessment of the current status. Any attempt to describe the individual and collective experiences of individuals inherently will be limited by the perspective of the writer. Especially with regard to lawyers currently practicing, short of conducting a survey, capturing the varied experiences of professionals is not possible. Every black lawyer has taken a unique route to becoming a lawyer and building a career, and this chapter does not attempt to describe them all.

Massachusetts as an Early Leader in Opportunities for Black Lawyers

Writing about black lawyers in Massachusetts up through the middle of the twentieth century is, in some sense, covering well-trod ground. J. Clay Smith's comprehensive survey, *Emancipation*, contains miniature biographies of the black lawyers whose careers represented key "firsts" for Massachusetts and, in many cases, the nation.[2] According to Smith's account, Macon Bolling Allen, who became the first black lawyer in the nation when he was admitted to practice in Maine in 1844, was the first black lawyer admitted to practice in Massachusetts in 1845.[3] His career provides an early illustration of the two overarching themes of the history of black lawyers in Massachusetts—the role of public service and seeking justice for blacks and the barriers they encountered as they sought to build a career. As Allen struggled to build a law practice, he was criticized by abolitionists in 1847 for refusing to sign a pledge against the war with Mexico. Abolitionists feared the war was a pretext for expanding slavery. Allen's response to this attack was to write to William Lloyd Garrison, publisher of *The Liberator*, to assert strong sympathies with his "brethren in bonds" and to state that he was "ever ready and willing to do all . . . for their amelioration." He concluded by stating that "[t]he cause of the Colored man, in whatever section of our country, expressly is really my own cause; and it would be monstrous indeed if I did not so regard it."[4] Allen initially was disappointed in his efforts to build a practice in Massachusetts after moving to Boston,[5] but was appointed a justice of the peace in 1847, which appointment was renewed in 1854. According to Smith, Allen's appointment as a justice of the peace made him the first black lawyer in the nation appointed to a judicial post.[6] Allen practiced law in Boston continuously until after the Civil War, when he relocated to Charleston, South Carolina.[7]

Robert Morris, Sr., admitted in Massachusetts in 1847, was the second black lawyer in the United States.[8] Morris became popular after winning a jury trial in the same year in possibly the first suit filed by a black lawyer. Because of his popularity after the trial, he was approached by Benjamin F. Roberts, who asked Morris to bring the case challenging racial segregation in Boston's public schools. Because of the requirement that "colored children" attend "colored schools," the plaintiff, Sarah Roberts, had to pass five schools on her way to the "colored school." Losing at the trial level, Morris had the assistance of future U.S. Senator Charles Sumner in filing an appeal in the case to the Supreme Judicial Court. The SJC's decision in the *Roberts* case infamously enshrined the concept of "separate but equal" into U.S. law, a concept not overturned until 105 years later by the U.S. Supreme Court in *Brown v. Board of Education*.[9]

Morris was involved in another case of national significance. In 1851, the U.S. marshal arrested a black waiter in Boston known as Frederick Wilkens, named in the warrant as Shadrack Minkins, under the Fugitive Slave Act of 1850. Morris represented Minkins. Accounts vary in the details, but agree that a crowd (variously described as black spectators or abolitionists), managed to extricate Minkins from control of the federal authorities and help him escape to Canada.[10] Accused of having had a role in orchestrating the escape, Morris and several other black citizens were indicted for treason and conspiracy to violate federal law. Found guilty in the first trial, the convictions were overturned by the appeals court. Morris was acquitted in a second trial in 1851. "Hence, a case that could have ended Morris's legal career instead increased his prestige among his people, the abolitionists, and the bar."[11]

Morris's role in the Minkins rescue was controversial among some who regarded it as a triumph of the mob over the rule of law.[12] Abolitionists were at odds with Boston conservatives and Southerners over enforcement of the Fugitive Slave Act. Despite the accusations of treason, the Massachusetts governor commissioned Morris as a magistrate in Essex County, making him the second black lawyer to hold a judicial post.[13] After the Civil War, Morris's private practice expanded, his popularity increased, and in 1866, he ran for mayor of Chelsea, albeit unsuccessfully.

Robert Morris's son, Robert Morris, Jr., also became a lawyer. Admitted in 1874, Robert Morris, Jr., became the first second-generation black lawyer in the nation. He died in 1883, two weeks after his father's death.[14]

The fourth black lawyer in Massachusetts, Edward Garrison Walker, was a skilled criminal law advocate after his admission in 1861. In 1866, Walker was elected to the Massachusetts General Court, the first black elected to a legislature in the United States.[15] Walker was a champion of women's suffrage while in the legislature, and in 1886, with Harris Wolff and Edward Everett Brown, formed the first black law firm in the nation.[16]

Even in the nineteenth century, law proved an attractive second career. In 1861, John Swett Rock, a black physician, left medicine for law. He became the first black lawyer admitted to the U.S. Supreme Court, appearing for admission on February 1, 1865, the day President Abraham Lincoln signed the joint resolution proposing the Thirteenth Amendment outlawing slavery.[17] Immediately following the admission ceremony, Dr. Rock was also received on the floor of the U.S. House of Representatives, another first for blacks. As Smith notes, Rock's admission to the Supreme Court bar was significant practically as well as symbolically. Excluding blacks from other courts as well as other civic rights was then difficult to justify.[18]

George Lewis Ruffin became the first black Harvard Law School graduate in 1869 and was elected to the Massachusetts state legislature from Boston in 1870, and was also elected to Boston's Common Council. Appointed a municipal judge in Charlestown in 1883, he served until his death in 1886.[19] Archibald Henry Grimké, an 1874 Harvard Law graduate, left law practice for journalism in 1887 in search of more lucrative work. President Grover Cleveland appointed him as U.S. consul in Santo Domingo in 1894.[20] Clement Garnett Morgan served on the Cambridge Common Council and as an alderman, and William Henry Lewis, Sr., won election to the Cambridge Common Council and later served in the Massachusetts House of Representatives. Lewis was appointed an assistant U.S. attorney in Boston in 1903 and held other federal office, including an appointment as assistant attorney general in 1911 by President Taft. After leaving the Department of Justice upon Woodrow Wilson's election in 1912, "[a]lthough he had sterling credentials, no apparent efforts were made to lure Lewis to any white law firms. He had simply been born too soon."[21] During the Wilson presidency, Lewis worked with other lawyers and scholars around the country to advocate for federal anti-lynching legislation. After leaving government service, he was in demand as a litigator, arguing cases before the U.S. Supreme Court.[22]

Edgar P. Benjamin became the first black graduate of Boston University School of Law in 1894 (he was admitted to the Massachusetts bar that same year). He built a practice representing attorneys and judges in mandamus proceedings, or who otherwise had legal problems.[23] After the turn of the twentieth century, black lawyers also established careers as lawyers in corporate legal offices. By 1920, Herman Emmon Moore and Julian D. Rainey had served on the legal staff of the Boston Elevated Railroad Corporation. Smith reports that Suffolk University Law School graduated its first black alumnus, Thomas Vreeland Jones, in 1915. Suffolk's second black graduate was Cyril Fitzgerald Butler, who completed his studies in 1919 and later became "a member of one of the first local legal committees established by the recently organized National Association for the Advancement of Colored People."[24]

About this time, black women began to enter the profession in small numbers.[25] Seventy-nine years after Macon Bolling Allen became the first black lawyer in Massachusetts, and forty-one years after Lelia J. Robinson became the first woman admitted to the Massachusetts bar, Blanche E. Braxton became the first black woman to gain admission to the Massachusetts bar in 1923 after graduating from Portia Law School.[26] In 1933, Braxton became the first black woman admitted to practice before the U.S. District Court in Massachusetts. Inez C. Fields, a 1922 Boston University School of Law graduate, followed her in 1924. Clara Burrill Bruce was the third black woman admitted in 1926 after serving as editor-in-chief of the *Boston University Law Review*—the first black student to head a law review in the history of legal education in the United States. Smith concludes his account of the careers of early black women lawyers in Massachusetts with a description of the career of Jacqueline Guild, a 1933 graduate of Portia Law School, who followed her father into practice in Cambridge. After her association with her father's firm ended, Smith reports that "[t]hereafter, her progress slowed, probably because of her race and sex, and her continued success in private practice began to wane."[27]

This overview of the careers of the experiences of some of the early black lawyers and judges in Massachusetts illustrates the connection between advocacy for the rights of blacks generally, and opportunities for advancement in the legal profession. Litigation efforts to end racial segregation in Boston schools in the 1840s, advocacy in opposition to attempts to enforce the Fugitive Slave Act, and the broader movement to abolish slavery up to the Civil War, and the efforts to secure civil rights for blacks after the war, involved black lawyers working together and with white colleagues on these important issues. This work—either legal work, or public advocacy—raised the public profiles of black lawyers and brought their qualifications to the attention of governors, presidents, and the electorate who chose the lawyers for judicial and other offices. While the intersection of race and sex presented special challenges for the black women who began entering the profession starting in the 1920s, black male lawyers encountered difficulties in building law practices and advancing their careers. J. Clay Smith's assessment that Jacqueline Guild's career prospects waned, while partially due to her sex, also aptly describes the less dramatic progress of blacks in the legal profession in Massachusetts in the first half of the twentieth century. Despite recording the early milestones—the first black lawyer in the nation, the first black members of the judiciary, the first black legislators, leading roles as litigators in the state and federal courts—further significant advancement for blacks in the legal profession awaited the galvanizing influence on the law and society of the Civil Rights Movement and advocacy on issues such as school desegregation required to make the legal gains of the movement real.

Blacks Slowly Gain Leadership in the Judiciary and Public Life in the Second Half of the Twentieth Century

As its title indicates, Smith's book covers the period until 1944. In the two decades immediately following, a few African Americans were appointed to judicial positions, notably G. Bruce Robinson to the Juvenile Court in 1948, Elwood S. McKenney to the District Court in 1960, and Joseph S. Mitchell to the Superior Court in 1966.

Massachusetts made history for the legal profession in 1962 when it elected Edward Brooke as the first black attorney general of Massachusetts and the first African American to serve any state in that role. Brooke achieved another "first" when he was elected to the U.S. Senate in 1966, the first black to serve in that body since Reconstruction. Brooke served in the Senate until 1979. Brooke rose to prominence in the Republican Party, but governors and leaders of both the Republican and Democratic parties have played a role in advancing the careers of black lawyers and adding diversity to the state and federal judiciary in Massachusetts. For example, recently, when Massachusetts Senator John Kerry was appointed by President Barack Obama to be secretary of state in 2013, Governor Deval Patrick appointed his legal counsel, William Maurice "Mo" Cowan, to fill the position until a special election could be held. Thus, Cowan became the second black to represent Massachusetts in the U.S. Senate.

The person responsible for appointing Cowan to the U.S. Senate, Deval Patrick, achieved a "first" himself when he was elected the seventy-first governor of Massachusetts and the first black governor in 2006, after a distinguished career in private practice, public service as assistant attorney general for civil rights in the U.S. Department of Justice, and as the chief legal officer of two major U.S. corporations—Texaco and the Coca-Cola Company. He is finishing his second term as this compilation goes to press and is not standing for reelection. His career certainly reflects the interrelationship between public service and achievement in the private sector. As discussions of recent milestone judicial appointments in Massachusetts make clear, Patrick has used this position, after a slow start, to appoint blacks and other underrepresented minorities to prominent positions in the judiciary—most notably his appointments of Roderick L. Ireland as chief justice, and Geraldine S. Hines as associate justice, of the Supreme Judicial Court (discussed further below).

The pace of change slowly accelerated after 1970. Harry J. Elam served on the Boston Municipal Court starting in 1971, and became chief justice of that court in 1978. He was elevated to the Superior Court in 1983. David S. Nelson was appointed to the Superior Court in 1973. In 1976, Frederick L. Brown became the first African American to serve on the Massachusetts Appeals Court, and in 1977, Margaret Burnham became the first black woman appointed to the judiciary when she became a judge on the Boston Municipal Court. Barbara A. Dortch-Okara was the first African-American woman appointed to the Superior Court in 1989 and became the first African American and woman to serve as the chief justice for Administration and Management of the Trial Court. She began her judicial service in 1984 on the Boston Municipal Court. Roderick L. Ireland made history when he became the first African American to serve on the Supreme Judicial Court, the state's highest court, in 1997, after having served on the Juvenile Court and the Appeals Court. Governor Patrick named Ireland chief justice in 2010. In 2014, Governor Patrick appointed Geraldine Hines to the Supreme Judicial Court, making her the first African-American woman to serve in that capacity. Even with these recent signal appointments, these "firsts" have been a long time in coming. The percentage of black judges serving in Massachusetts courts currently hovers at the 8 percent mark.[28]

In the federal court realm, David S. Nelson made the transition from the state Superior Court to the federal District Court when he was appointed to the U.S. District Court for Massachusetts in 1979. That same year Joyce London Alexander became the first African-American federal magistrate judge. From 1996 to 1999, she served as chief magistrate judge for the District of Massachusetts. Reginald C. Lindsay was appointed to succeed David Nelson in 1993 after Nelson's death in 1991 at age sixty-five. Lindsay served until his untimely death in 2009. The U.S.

District Court has created living memorials to both men for their pioneering roles in the federal courts in Massachusetts. The Nelson Fellowship Program is a summer program for twelve public school students in Boston, Springfield, Worcester, and Brockton, and offers the opportunity for the fellow to participate in the work of a judge's chambers, to benefit from structured classes, and to meet community leaders and learn about local colleges and the college application process.[29] Every year the Lindsay Fellowship Program selects five or six college students interested in pursuing a career in law who participate in intensive educational opportunities to develop research and writing skills and an understanding of the work of federal prosecutors and public defenders.[30] These two programs work to ensure that the pipeline of young people entering the legal profession contains a robust representation of blacks and other minorities.

President Barack Obama cured the lack of representation of African-American women on the federal courts serving Massachusetts in 2010 by appointing Denise Jefferson Casper as the first African-American woman to serve as a federal district judge in Massachusetts. The same year, Rhode Island attorney O. Rogeriee Thompson became the first African American and the second woman to serve as a judge on the U.S. Court of Appeals for the First Circuit. While these appointments are significant in breaking barriers, for the U.S. District Court in Massachusetts, one among the sixteen judges is African American, and only one among the ten judges of the Court of Appeals for the First Circuit is African American.

African-American women lawyers have also achieved in the political sphere. Dianne Wilkerson is the only African-American woman to have served in the Massachusetts Senate,[31] and Marie St. Fleur became the first Haitian-American to hold elective office in Massachusetts when she was elected a state representative in 1999.[32] Andrea Cabral was the first female in the Commonwealth's history to serve as sheriff of Suffolk County (she is currently the state secretary of public safety).

Although the case brought by Robert Morris, Sr., the second black lawyer in Massachusetts, eliminated legally sanctioned segregation in Boston's public schools, Boston returned to efforts to desegregate its public schools 120 years later, in 1970. In the case of *Morgan v. Hennigan*, parents of black children alleged that the Boston School Committee violated the equal protection clause of the Fourteenth Amendment to the U.S. Constitution through a deliberate policy of operating racially segregated schools. One of the lawyers challenging the policy was Thomas I. Atkins, who was the first African American elected to the Boston City Council in the twentieth century in 1967. In 1974, the federal court, in a ruling unanimously affirmed by the First Circuit, ordered the desegregation of the schools through new student assignment, teacher employment, and facility improvement measures, as well as busing.[33] The resistance to the implementation of the school assignment and busing orders in Boston's white neighborhoods and the associated violence tarnished Boston's reputation and has had lasting repercussions for the ability to recruit black and African-American lawyers to build careers in Massachusetts.

Twentieth Anniversary of the
Equal Justice Report

The publication of this book coincides with the twentieth anniversary of the release of *Equal Justice: Eliminating the Barriers*, the final report of the Commission to Study Racial and Ethnic Bias in the Courts established by the Supreme Judicial Court.[34] At the time of that report 8.8 percent of Massachusetts trial court judges were people of color. While these numbers certainly have improved, progress continues to be slow. As of July 1, 2014, thirty-three of the 411 authorized judgeship positions in Massachusetts are held by African Americans, representing just over 8 percent of the total.[35] Forty-nine judges are American Indian, African American, Hispanic, or Asian, representing 11.9 percent of the total, so some modest improvement has occurred since 1994. In roughly the same time period, the percentage of minority law school graduates overall has increased from about 14 percent to over 25 percent.[36] The *Equal Justice* report also identified perceptions that the judicial selection process is biased against minority attorneys and that minorities were primarily considered for courts serving large minority populations, noting both underrepresentation of minorities on gubernatorial screening panels and a sense that minority judicial applicants were held to higher standards in the screening process.[37] The recent improvement in the numbers of black judges and appointments to the state's appellate courts indicates progress in the intervening twenty years—that governors have taken the message of the report seriously. Recently, concerns have been raised that racism may taint the process for attorneys to evaluate judges.[38] These reports seem to echo the findings of the 1994 Supreme Judicial Court report that minority attorneys often receive poor treatment from other attorneys and suffer negative perceptions of the professionalism of minority attorneys.[39] As in other areas of the legal system and society, unconscious or implicit bias is a barrier preventing lawyers and judges of color from attaining full equality in their professional roles.

Black Lawyers in Private Practice and Corporate Law Offices

The representation of black or African-American lawyers in large law firms, similar to representation in the judiciary, reflects disappointing progress. The election of Richard A. Soden as a partner at Goodwin Procter LLP in 1979,[40] followed by Harry T. Daniels at the firm known as Hale and Dorr in 1981,[41] and Roscoe Trimmier, Jr., at Ropes & Gray in 1983,[42] seemed to be evidence of an auspicious trend. Each was the first black partner at his firm. Soden is now retired, serving as counsel with Goodwin, while Daniels and Trimmier have fully retired. When Trimmier retired in 2009, three African-American partners remained at the firm, among them Diane Patrick, the wife of Deval Patrick. A similar situation prevails at all of Boston's largest firms. Nationally, about 7.1 percent of partners are minorities and 2.26 percent of partners are minority women. Minorities account for 21 percent of associates and 22 percent of staff attorneys, and minority women are represented at 11.3 percent among associates and 14.4 percent among staff attorneys. For the Boston area, 2.7 percent of associates are black and 1.27 percent are black women. At the partnership level, blacks represent 0.92 percent of partners, and 0.20 percent are black women.[43]

In a profile published as Trimmier anticipated his retirement from Ropes & Gray in 2009, the *Boston Business Journal* mentioned "several different factors" that have made Boston "a tough city to thrive in for minority lawyers, including the scarce pipeline of minorities, a business climate in Boston that has been described as hostile, and, more recently, the economy."[44] Other black lawyers quoted in the article noted Boston's reputation for being "less than welcoming to lawyers of color." A 2002 *Boston Globe* article noted that "many minorities avoided the city because of [Boston's] reputation for racial strife during the tensions during court-ordered busing to work toward desegregating the public schools."[45] Another factor is the difficulty any lawyer faces in making partner and the long path to partnership.

Ralph Martin, who was then the managing partner of Bingham McCutchen LLP and who, since 2011, has been senior vice president and general counsel for Northeastern University, commented on "invisible barriers . . . that exist in a meritocracy" and stated that "[i]f you don't devise systems to help with the elimination of those invisible barriers, inevitably your attrition rate for lawyers of color and women will be higher than it is for majority males."[46] As an aside, Martin's career path included serving as district attorney for Suffolk County from 1992 to 2002. Another black partner serving as a firm's leader is Steven Wright, who is the executive partner overseeing the Boston office of Holland & Knight.

Another trailblazer among black lawyers has been Wayne Budd, who served as U.S. attorney for the District of Massachusetts from 1989 to 1992; in 1992 he was appointed associate attorney general in the U.S. Department of Justice, echoing the career of William Henry Lewis, Sr., in the first decade of the twentieth century. Unlike Lewis, however, Budd had many opportunities in the private sector after leaving government service.[47] He was a partner at Goodwin Procter from 1993 to 1996. He served as a member of the board of directors and as senior executive vice president and general counsel at John Hancock Financial Services, Inc., and had been group president–New England of the Bell Atlantic Corporation, now

Verizon Communications. Budd rejoined Goodwin in 2004 as senior counsel. Like Deval Patrick, Budd's career has included government service, law firm practice, and experience in corporate counsel positions. While at John Hancock, Budd made diversity "a critical factor in selecting legal representation."[48]

Other African Americans who have served leading institutions in in-house counsel positions are Brent Henry at Partners Healthcare and Stephanie Lovell, who has held senior positions in the Massachusetts Attorney General's Office and is now general counsel at Blue Cross Blue Shield of Massachusetts after having served in a similar capacity at Boston Medical Center.

Women lawyers lagged men in attaining partnerships in major firms numerically and in time. Ruth Ellen Fitch was the first African-American woman to become a partner at a major Boston law firm when she became partner at Palmer & Dodge, now known as Edwards Wildman Palmer, in 1991. In addition to Diane Patrick at Ropes & Gray, Essence McGill Arzu, at Foley Hoag, and Paulette Brown, at Edwards Wildman Palmer, are other woman African-American partners at major Boston firms.

Geraldine Hines, Margaret Burnham, and Judith Dilday are black women lawyers who have secured their places in history as members of the judiciary. They also were the founding partners of a minority women's law firm in 1989.[49] This firm was a visible manifestation of how black lawyers have worked through smaller private firms to build professional careers.

Blacks in Academia

Legal education is another robust component of the legal profession in Massachusetts. As with representation in the large law firms and overall in the profession, despite some notable successes, African Americans remain underrepresented in the legal academy. Derrick Bell became the first black tenured professor at Harvard Law School in 1971. C. Clyde Ferguson, who came from a distinguished career as a diplomat and authority on human rights in international law and dean of Howard Law

School, joined the Harvard Law faculty in 1977. He was named to the Henry L. Stimson chair in 1981, before his untimely death at age fifty-nine in 1983. Randall L. Kennedy, the Michael R. Klein Professor of Law, joined the Harvard Law faculty in 1984, followed in 1986 by David B. Wilkins, currently vice dean of Global Initiatives on the Legal Profession, director of the Program on the Legal Profession, and the Lester Kissel Professor of Law, who has conducted valuable research on the experience of blacks and other minorities in the legal profession. Harvard Law School did not add a black woman to its tenured faculty until 1998, when Lani Guinier moved to Harvard from the University of Pennsylvania. This appointment followed several years of protest by Derrick Bell, who ultimately lost his position at Harvard because of the protest. Ruth Arlene Howe, who arrived at Boston College Law School as a student in 1970, was the first African American to achieve the rank of full professor at that institution. Margaret Burnham, the first African-American woman appointed to any court in Massachusetts, is now on the faculty at Northeastern University School of Law.

In recent years, several African Americans have served as deans of Massachusetts law schools. Robert V. Ward, Jr., became dean at Southern New England School of Law in North Dartmouth in 1999 and led the transition of the school to its current form as the University of Massachusetts School of Law in 2010. Camille Nelson became the first woman and black to serve as dean of Suffolk University Law School when she was appointed to the position in 2010. Vincent C. Rogeau became the first African-American dean of Boston College Law School in 2011.

The Role of Black Lawyers in Bar Associations

As I noted in an earlier work, one reason black lawyers were able to make progress in the law despite their exclusion from bar organizations was the ability to combine their talents and resources.[50] These organizations provided networks from which black lawyers could advocate for legal issues affecting their communities and to advocate for the advancement of black lawyers in private practice and in the public sphere.

The Massachusetts Black Lawyers' Association (MBLA) formed in 1973 and now has a forty-year legacy of successful advocacy. The Massachusetts Black Women Attorneys (MBWA) is of similar vintage—and formed in recognition that black women lawyers may encounter unique challenges different from, and perhaps in addition to, the obstacles confronting black men in the profession.[51] As well as providing forums for advocacy, the MBLA and MBWA gave African-American lawyers leadership opportunities and occasions to attain individual visibility. Blacks have attained leadership positions in Boston Bar Association (BBA) and Massachusetts Bar Association (MBA). Rudolph F. Pierce became the first African-American president of the BBA in 1989 and Richard Soden followed in 1995. This author became the first African-American woman and the first legal academic to lead the BBA in 2003. Wayne Budd was the first African-American president of the MBA in 1979 and, at age thirty-eight, was the youngest president of any state bar association at the time. James S. Dilday also served as MBA president from 1995 to 1996. In 2014, Paulette Brown, a partner in the Boston law firm of Edwards Wildman Palmer LLP, became president-elect of the American Bar Association, and in 2015 she will become the first African-American woman to lead the organization, which effectively excluded blacks from membership until 1943.[52]

Surveying the Past and Scanning the Horizon

This chapter began with a recognition that the history of black lawyers in Massachusetts and the contemporary concerns of black lawyers are well-trod ground. Writings range from careful chronicles of the first African Americans to reach certain professional goals, to celebrations of the progress these attainments represent, to examinations of the barriers explicit and subtle that impede rapid and more widespread progress, and laments of the leakages in the pipelines feeding the future of the law schools and the legal profession. Each of these perspectives is important to learn and understand. The black lawyers whose accomplishments are mentioned by name all have made amazing contributions to the advancement of the law and have made the path to success easier for others in the profession. Their work is worthy of celebration.

Perhaps because Massachusetts abolished slavery by 1783, it was able to record many "firsts" in the advancement of blacks in the legal profession. Based on this early headstart over much of the nation, one would expect great progress toward equality in the professional achievements of lawyers and in all realms of society. The modern record, while evidencing progress, disappoints.

After the individual milestones of the nineteenth century for male lawyers and in the early twentieth century for women lawyers, advancement along the path of achievement seems to stall until the end of World War II, only really picking up steam at the time of the Civil Rights Movement in the 1960s. The achievements in representation of blacks in the judiciary, in public service, and in law firms are important. Because of the visibility of positions in public service, it is unlikely that progress will be greatly slowed. That so little progress can be measured in the racial composition of the Massachusetts judiciary in the twenty years since the racial and ethnic bias study of the courts is, however, concerning. But the resistance to real change in private law firms and other less visible sectors gives cause for additional concern. That the pioneering black partners in major Boston law firms would retire without being able to look back on a consistent stream of successors is tragic. The message is that the profession is content with tokenism. As I wrote in a *Boston Bar Journal* article in 2006, the failure to achieve any other business goal would be a crisis for most firms—failure to achieve diversity goals is met with a shrug. I do not doubt that some efforts have been sincere, but in the end, results matter. No doubt, progress has been confounded by the economic crisis that has especially afflicted the legal profession since 2008—but any recovery must not be at the expense of forward progress toward true diversity in the profession.

I ended my survey of the history on the positive note of Paulette Brown's ascension to leadership in the American Bar Association. Her role builds on the history related here of lawyers working to advance blacks in the profession while improving the nation's adherence to its aspirations of equality. Massachusetts should be proud of its early history and continued progress, but the private bar and the public sector should work to ensure that the path over the horizon measures up to the promising record of the early beginnings.

Timeline of Selected Notable Persons and Events

1845	Macon Bolling Allen is the first African American admitted to the Massachusetts bar.
1883	George Lewis Ruffin becomes the first African-American judge in Massachusetts when he is appointed to the Charlestown Municipal Court.
1910	African-American lawyer Butler R. Wilson is a charter member of the Massachusetts Bar Association.
1923	Blanche E. Braxton is the first African-American woman admitted to the Massachusetts bar.
1924	Clara Burrill Bruce, a student at Boston University School of Law, becomes the first African American to serve as editor-in-chief of a law review.
1973	The Massachusetts Black Lawyers' Association is founded.
1977	Margaret Burnham becomes the first African-American woman judge in Massachusetts when she is appointed to the Boston Municipal Court.
1991	Ruth Ellen Fitch is the first African-American woman to become a partner at a major Boston law firm when she makes partner at Palmer & Dodge (now Edwards Wildman Palmer LLP).
1997	Roderick L. Ireland is sworn in as the first African-American associate justice of the Supreme Judicial Court. (He becomes the court's first African-American chief justice in 2010.)
2014	Geraldine S. Hines is the first African-American woman appointed to the Supreme Judicial Court.

Endnotes

[1] J. Clay Smith, Jr., *Emancipation: The Making of the Black Lawyer, 1844–1944*, at 114 (1993) [hereinafter Smith, *Emancipation*]. *See generally* David B. Wilkins, "Doing Well By Doing Good? The Role of Public Service in the Careers of Black Corporate Lawyers," 41 *Houston L. Rev.* 1 (2004).

[2] *See generally* Smith, *Emancipation* at 93–125. (The second chapter of the book is entitled "New England: The Genesis of the Black Lawyer." Most of the lawyers discussed are Massachusetts lawyers.) For an online source of information about the history of participation of African-American judges and lawyers and Massachusetts, see Massachusetts Historical Society, *Long Road to Justice: The African American Experience in the Massachusetts Courts, available at* http://www.masshist.org/longroad/index.htm. This source contains short biographical sketches of selected lawyers and judges from the mid-nineteenth century through the early twenty-first century.

[3] Smith, *Emancipation* at 94. Some evidence exists that William Henry Johnson may have been the first African American eligible to practice law because he had qualified for the bar in 1842, but he was not sworn in until 1865. From *Slave Quarters to the Courtroom: The Story of the First African American Attorney in the United States, available at* http://www.blackpast.org/perspectives/william-henry-squire-johnson-slave-quarters-courtroom. Johnson, who was born into slavery in Virginia, escaped to New Bedford in 1833. He studied law while working as a janitor in a law office. Some speculate that because he was technically a fugitive slave, he could not become a practicing attorney. *Slave Quarters to the Courtroom.* He was active as a speaker in the anti-slavery movement and the Temperance Movement, even though he later represented liquor dealers. *Slave Quarters to the Courtroom.* Smith also discusses Johnson's career. Smith, *Emancipation* at 102.

[4] Smith, *Emancipation* at 95.

[5] Smith, *Emancipation* at 95 (citing letter from Allen to John Jay of Nov. 26, 1845).

[6] Smith, *Emancipation* at 96.

[7] Smith, *Emancipation* at 96.

[8] Smith, *Emancipation* at 96.

[9] Smith, *Emancipation* at 97; *Roberts v. City of Boston*, 59 Mass. 198 (1849). For another account of the circumstances of the *Roberts* case, see Barbara F. Berenson, *Boston and the Civil War: Hub of the Second Revolution* 35–37 (2014) [hereinafter Berenson, *Boston and the Civil War*]. The Massachusetts legislature abolished formal segregation in schools in 1855. Berenson, *Boston and the Civil War* at 37.

[10] Smith, *Emancipation* at 98; Berenson, *Boston and the Civil War* at 50–51.

[11] Smith, *Emancipation* at 99; Berenson, *Boston and the Civil War* at 50–51.

[12] Smith, *Emancipation* at 98–99; Berenson, *Boston and the Civil War* at 51.

[13] Smith, *Emancipation* at 99.

[14] Smith, *Emancipation* at 99–100.

[15] Smith, *Emancipation* at 100. Walker may share this honor with a Vermont man elected to the state legislature in the same year.

[16] Smith, *Emancipation* at 100.

[17] Smith, *Emancipation* at 100–01.

[18] Smith, *Emancipation* at 102 (quoting Charles Sumner on the significance of Rock's admission).

[19] Smith, *Emancipation* at 103.

[20] Smith, *Emancipation* at 104.

[21] Smith, *Emancipation* at 107.

[22] Smith, *Emancipation* at 105–08.

[23] Smith, *Emancipation* at 109.

[24] Smith, *Emancipation* at 110.

[25] Smith, *Emancipation* at 111. For a description of the history of women lawyers of color in Massachusetts, including black lawyers, see Renée M. Landers, "Invisibility, Isolations and Resilience: Women Lawyers of Color, The Inchoate Journey of Leadership and Service of Women Lawyers of Color in Massachusetts," in *Breaking Barriers: The Unfinished Story of Women Lawyers and Judges in Massachusetts* 140–52 and personal reflections of selected lawyers at 152–58 (Pattie B. Saris, Margot Botsford, and Barbara F. Berenson, eds., MCLE, Inc. 2012) [hereinafter *Breaking Barriers*].

[26] Smith, *Emancipation* at 111. [27] Smith, *Emancipation* at 111. For a description of Leila J. Robinson's career, see *Breaking Barriers* at 4–5.

[28] Matt Viser, "Governor picks fewer minorities for bench," *The Boston Globe*, Dec. 5, 2008, at A-1. See, *infra*, text and notes at nn.35 & 36.

[29] *See* http://www.mad.uscourts.gov/outreach/nelson.htm.

[30] *See* http://www.mad.uscourts.gov/outreach/lindsay.htm.

[31] Wilkerson resigned the Senate seat in 2008 after being indicted on corruption charges. She pleaded guilty to several charges in 2010. Matt Viser, "Facing possible expulsion, Wilkerson quits Senate," *The Boston Globe*, Nov. 20, 2008, at A-1 (cited in *Breaking Barriers* at 162 n.55).

[32] St. Fleur resigned in 2010 to take a position with the City of Boston. Travis Anderson, "Rep. St. Fleur to take City hall job," *The Boston Globe*, Apr. 24, 2010, at B.1 (cited in *Breaking Barriers* 162 n.56).

[33] *See* http://www.masshist.org/longroad/02education/morgan.htm.

[34] Supreme Judicial Court, *Commission to Study Racial and Ethnic Bias in the Courts*, Final Report (1994).

[35] Supreme Judicial Court Public Information Office, Chart, Number of Judges in Massachusetts Courts by Court, Gender and Race, July 1, 2014 (on file with the author).

[36] NALP Bulletin, *Increasing Diversity of Law School Graduates Not Reflected Among Judicial Clerks*, September 2014 (citing statistics from 1993 and 2013). This report noted that "the overall representation of minorities among judicial clerks has increased only marginally since the mid-1990s and has essentially flat-lined over the past ten years. The representation has declined for Blacks/African Americans." These statistics are concerning because judicial clerkships are gateways to elite positions in the legal profession.

[37] Smith, *Emancipation* at 102–03.

[38] Adrian Walker, "Evidence of bias against black judges," *The Boston Globe*, June 11, 2014, *available at* http://www.bostonglobe.com/metro/2014/06/10/judging-judges-effort-address-racial-bias-judicial-reviews-has-created-racial-firestorm-bench/Iq3x11bGAJuDWJbsIGLkpM/story.html.

[39] Supreme Judicial Court, *Commission to Study Racial and Ethnic Bias in the Courts*, Final Report 117–21 (1994).

[40] *See* http://www.goodwinprocter.com/People/S/Soden-Richard.aspx.

[41] The firm is now known as Wilmer Cutler Pickering Hale and Dorr LLP, or "Wilmer Hale." *See* http://www.wilmerhale.com/harry_daniels.

[42] Lisa van der Pool, *Pioneer's Lament: A Trail-blazing Black Partner Laments Dearth of Successors*, available at http://www.bizjournals.com/boston/stories/2009/11/16/story2.html.

[43] All statistics are from NALP Bulletin, *Women and Minorities at Law Firms by Race and Ethnicity—An Update*, February 2014, collected from employers listed in the 2013–2014 *NALP Directory of Legal Employers*.

[44] Lisa van der Pool, *Pioneer's Lament: A Trail-blazing Black Partner Laments Dearth of Successors*, available at http://www.bizjournals.com/boston/stories/2009/11/16/story2.html.

[45] Diane E. Lewis, "Faces of Color at Law Firms Are Rare Boston's Legacy of Racial Strife Makes Recruiting Tougher," *The Boston Globe*, July 7, 2002.

[46] Diane E. Lewis, "Faces of Color at Law Firms Are Rare Boston's Legacy of Racial Strife Makes Recruiting Tougher," *The Boston Globe*, July 7, 2002.

[47] See endnote 21, above, for a discussion of the career of William Henry Lewis, Sr.

[48] Diane E. Lewis, "Faces of Color at Law Firms Are Rare Boston's Legacy of Racial Strife Makes Recruiting Tougher," *The Boston Globe*, July 7, 2002.

[49] John H. Kennedy, "Another Barrier Broken Boston's Newest Law Firm Has Only Black Women as Partners," *The Boston Globe*, Dec. 2, 1989, at 11. Margaret Burnham, as noted earlier, was the first African-American woman appointed to any court in Massachusetts when she was appointed to the Boston Municipal Court in 1977. Geraldine Hines served on the Superior Court and the Massachusetts Appeals Court before her appointment to the Supreme Judicial Court in 2014. Judith Nelson Dilday retired from the Probate and Family Court in 2009 after becoming the first African American to serve as a judge in 1993. *See* Landers, *Breaking Barriers* at 162 n.57.

[50] *Breaking Barriers* at 149 and 162 n.58.

[51] Commission on Women in the Profession, American Bar Association, *Visible Invisibility: Women of Color in Law Firms* 2 (2006) (citing American Bar Association, Multicultural Women Attorneys Network, *The Burdens of Both, The Privileges of Neither* 6, 9 (1994)). In 2008, the ABA released a follow-up publication to the 2006 study, *From Visible Invisibility to Visibly Successful: Success Strategies for Law Firms and Women of Color in Law Firms*, based on interviews with twenty-eight women of color.

[52] *Breaking Barriers* at 162 n.58; *see* Katie Johnston, "Equity Partner: Paulette Brown, who has championed diversity in the legal profession, becomes the first black woman to lead the American Bar Association," *Boston Sunday Globe*, Sept. 7, 2014, at G-1, G-5.

———

The Experience of Women Lawyers

Susan M. Finegan, Esq.
Jennifer Mather McCarthy, Esq.

Introduction

This chapter has been adapted from Virginia G. Drachman, "From the Pioneers to the New Women," and Rebecca Rogers and Sarah Wald, "Women and the Judiciary in Massachusetts, Then and Now," in *Breaking Barriers: The Unfinished Story of Women Lawyers and Judges in Massachusetts* (MCLE, Inc. 2012).[1] The authors extend their gratitude to those three women for their original and inspiring work.

The First Women Lawyers in Massachusetts

In 1888 Lelia J. Robinson, the first woman admitted to the Massachusetts bar, offered women advice on how to succeed in the legal profession. "Do not take sex into the practice. Don't be 'lady lawyers.' Simply be lawyers, and recognize no distinction—no existence of any distinction between yourselves and the other members of the bar. . . . You can take this stand and yet in no wise cease to be ladies—true ladies in every sense of the word." Mary Anne Greene, Robinson's friend and "sister in law," and the second woman admitted to practice law in the Commonwealth, took a different tack. While Robinson made the argument for gender equality, Greene highlighted the importance of gender difference, claiming that women's unique sympathies gave them a special place in the legal profession. Greene envisioned law as an ideal "field for women" because "just as many women would prefer to consult a woman physician because they could talk freely and be more sure of sympathy, so they would, for the same reasons, consult a woman lawyer."

Despite their accomplishments as pioneer women lawyers in Massachusetts, neither Robinson nor Greene could forget that she was a woman in a male-dominated profession. Indeed, the nineteenth-century woman lawyer straddled two worlds. As a woman, her place was at home, the caretaker of the family. As a lawyer, her place was in the office and the courtroom, the protector of justice. As a woman, she was expected to be modest, sentimental, and caring. As a lawyer, she needed to be assertive and logical. The challenge was not unique to Robinson and Greene. One nineteenth-century woman lawyer identified this conflict between gender and professional identity as the burden of "double consciousness" that confronted every "woman who wishes to be a lawyer." This dilemma of double consciousness endured long after Robinson and the women of her generation had overcome the institutional obstacles necessary to practice law in Massachusetts.

The history of women lawyers in Massachusetts begins with Lelia J. Robinson, the first woman to graduate from Boston University School of Law, in 1881, and, as noted above, the first woman admitted to the

Massachusetts bar, in 1882. Mary Greene followed Robinson, graduating second in her law school class at Boston University in 1888 and gaining admission to the bar of Suffolk County that year, ranking first among approximately forty applicants. By 1890, eight women were studying law at Boston University and several others were reading law in offices. Numbers tell only part of the story; behind the growth of women lawyers in Massachusetts is a more complicated history. On the one hand, it is a story of women's struggles to break barriers and overcome gender discrimination as they strived to make it in the legal profession. At the same time, it is a personal story of women trying to blaze professional paths without sacrificing their traditional domestic responsibilities. The history of the first half-century of women lawyers in Massachusetts reveals the origins and development of the dilemma of double consciousness, a struggle that persists today.

As the first woman lawyer in Massachusetts, Lelia Robinson encountered both obstacles and opportunities. The elite law schools in the Northeast—Harvard, Columbia, Yale, and the University of Pennsylvania—were all closed to women. In contrast, law schools in the western part of the country were more hospitable to women. The University of Iowa and Washington University in St. Louis opened their doors to women in 1868, the newly founded law school at the University of Michigan opened to women in 1870, and Ada Kepley graduated from Union College of Law (now Northwestern University School of Law) in 1870 to become the first woman in the country to earn a law degree. As the trend toward coeducation in law schools spread in the west, Boston University bucked the tide in the east. When it opened its doors in 1872 to both men and women, it gave women access to the first law school in the country that required an admission exam before entry as well as a three-year course of instruction.

Robinson enrolled at Boston University School of Law in 1878 and graduated fourth in her class. Despite her superior record, she confronted obstacles daily as she negotiated the delicate task of being the only woman among 150 male classmates. "I knew none of the students, and the dean, to whom I introduced myself, did not give me any introductions to students or professors." Left to make her own way, Robinson sat up front in her classes, unaware of the tradition of alphabetical seating. She shunned the demure behavior expected of a proper lady of her day, resolved to be friendly and outgoing with her male classmates, and ultimately won them over. "I was not permitted to realize or remember the fact that I was the only woman in a large school of men," Robinson recalled proudly. "I was simply a student like the rest."

After graduating with honors from Boston University School of Law, the first female graduate of the school, Robinson was denied admission to the state bar because she was a woman. In response, Robinson sued to establish the right of a woman to practice law, and while she lost in court, she nevertheless secured her victory when Massachusetts adopted a statute specifically permitting women to practice law on the same terms as men.[2] In 1882, Robinson became the first woman lawyer admitted to practice in the state, crossing, as she put it, "the grand Rubicon which made me a full fledged attorney." Robinson's admission was an important victory in the history of the pioneer generation of women lawyers in Massachusetts, but she quickly realized that it was only the first step. No one in Boston would hire the first woman lawyer in the state, so she opened her own office. She tried to build a practice for three and a half years, but "business came in very slowly . . . and consisted mostly of small and rather hopeless claims for collection." Robinson finally faced the hard truth that she could not make it as a woman lawyer in Boston and turned her sights to the west, where she had heard that views on women were more liberal than they were in the Northeast.

Lured by the promise of more open attitudes toward women, Robinson moved to Seattle where she found open doors that were tightly shut in Boston. A male judge befriended her and encouraged her to do courtroom work, something she had dreaded back in Boston. To help her get started, he appointed her as counsel for a prisoner. "With fear and trembling," Robinson defended her client before a judge and jury, and learned firsthand that she "could do the work" she had deemed the sole domain of her male colleagues in Boston. Quickly, she established a lucrative law practice that combined office and courtroom work, but after barely a year, she gave it all up and went back to Boston in 1888 to be near her family.

Robinson returned home a more confident and experienced lawyer. She opened an office at 5 Pemberton Square, near the newly completed Suffolk County Courthouse, and built a modest practice. Robinson was also delighted to find a small group of women lawyers who had gained admission to practice in Massachusetts while she was away. "These ladies have helped to accustom our good old conservative Boston to the thought of women in the legal profession." Among this group of women lawyers were Mary Greene and Anna Christy Fall, both of whom had managed to establish successful careers. Greene found encouragement and opportunity from a prominent Boston lawyer, Alfred Hemenway, who opened his office to her, enabling her to "learn what I could of office work," while lending his prestige to the cause of women lawyers in Massachusetts. Anna Christy Fall, another honors student at Boston University School of Law, was admitted to the bar in 1891. In search of community among this group of local women lawyers, Robinson organized the Portia Club, and invited Greene, Fall, and the several women law students at Boston University to meet monthly at a downtown hotel for dinner and conversation. Robinson and Greene also joined the Equity Club, a correspondence club for women lawyers around the country.

Robinson's and Greene's letters to their "sisters in law" in the Equity Club make clear that these two pioneer women lawyers of Massachusetts struggled with the dilemma of double consciousness that challenged all women lawyers of their day. Double consciousness touched every aspect of nineteenth-century women lawyers' professional lives: the type of practice they chose; their relationship to social reform; whether they worked in an office or ventured into the courtroom; and, if they went to court, how they should dress.

In this era when women belonged at home, women lawyers debated their proper place in the profession. Some, like Robinson, believed that a woman lawyer was more suited to the office than the courtroom. The office was a private workplace, like the home, and demanded the skills familiar to a housewife—detail, organization, efficiency, and compromise.

In contrast, the courtroom resembled a saloon, with its spittoons and the presence of thieves, murderers, and prostitutes. Here, in the public eye, male lawyers engaged in legal combat, flaunting their manly qualities— combativeness, competitiveness, and hard-hearted objectivity. "I very emphatically chose office practice," explained Robinson, who often referred her litigation cases to male lawyers to avoid the hostile atmosphere of the courtroom. Greene disagreed, arguing not only that a woman lawyer belonged in the courtroom, but that "the less agreeable the moral atmosphere" of the courtroom, "the more is her presence needed."

Despite their differing views on women in the courtroom, both Robinson and Greene occasionally went to court, where they confronted another challenge of double consciousness, namely, the perplexing problem of the hat. Robinson raised the issue with the Equity Club members in 1888 when she had to take a case to court for the first time. "Shall the woman attorney wear her hat when arguing a case or making a motion in court, or shall she remove it?" Robinson wanted to know. Despite the larger and more difficult challenges Robinson had confronted as she fought to overcome barriers against women lawyers in Massachusetts, her query was no frivolous matter of fashion. Social etiquette of the day required that respectable women wear hats in public, but professional, male standards demanded that lawyers remove their hats in the courtroom. Robinson and Greene, as well as "the ladies who are at present studying law" all preferred to wear a hat in court. Greene observed, "The matter seems to be settled in Massachusetts in the affirmative."

Even as Robinson and Greene resolved the dilemma of the hat for themselves, double consciousness permeated their personal lives, confronting them with the more enduring tension between marriage and career. Again, Robinson put her finger on the problem. In 1889, as she published a book on family law, *The Law of Husband and Wife*, and contemplated her own marriage, Robinson turned once more to the women lawyers of the Equity Club for advice. "Is it practicable for a woman to successfully fulfill the duties of wife, mother and lawyer at the same time? Especially a young married woman?" In an era before the availability of reliable methods of birth control, Robinson understood all too well that she would never be free to build her professional career until the arrangements of her personal life were well in order. For some women, the answer to Robinson's question was simple: women had to choose between career and marriage. Greene, for one, remained single, and devoted her time to her career. Still, even as a single woman, she found that household responsibilities intruded on her work. Explaining that she had to "sandwich law and housekeeping together," Greene lamented that she could not "practice just as a man does."

Robinson took a different path. In 1890, she married Eli Sawtelle, a piano dealer, who was supportive of his new wife's career. Robinson's decision to marry Sawtelle reflected the understanding among nine-teenth-century women lawyers that the key to managing career and marriage was finding the right man. Women lawyers need not fear marriage, explained one woman lawyer in Chicago, "but it makes all the difference in the world who one marries." Sawtelle's wedding gift to his new wife was a "fine roll-top desk" for her office, and he willingly took time out of their honeymoon trip so that she could be admitted to the U.S. Supreme Court in Washington, DC. Anna Christy Fall married a lawyer and went into practice with him. With her husband's support, Fall took cases to court. In November 1891, she became the first woman to try a jury case in the Commonwealth, winning her case against "one of the ablest and most noted lawyers of Massachusetts." A mother of two young children early in her practice, Fall did not let motherhood hinder her court-room career, even when she was nursing. Instead, her sister or a domestic servant brought the baby to court at a scheduled feeding time. The judge, in the face of Boston's conservative reputation, usually granted a recess at Fall's request, and she quickly retreated into the witness room to nurse before resuming her position before the bench.

Although the prevailing view in the late nineteenth century was that women must choose between marriage and career, Robinson and Fall were testimony to the fact that for the pioneer generation of women lawyers, marriage to a supportive husband could encourage and nourish a woman lawyer's public career. At the same time, even the happiest married women lawyers were not unaffected by the expectations of domesticity and sacrifice that defined the parameters of proper womanhood in their day. While Robinson's husband barely complained when "every pair of socks is in need of mending," Robinson would "sit down the same instant, usually, and have a pair ready in about three minutes." Still, she felt that even that may not have been enough. "I think I haven't neglected my husband, but am not quite certain even of that," she confessed privately to another woman lawyer.

In 1890, the year of her marriage, Robinson published an essay in the law journal *Green Bag*, entitled "Women Lawyers in the United States." Although she was well aware of the obstacles that women lawyers faced as they headed toward the twentieth century, her essay was a celebration of women lawyers' accomplishments in the late nineteenth century and concluded with the optimistic claim that women would continue to enter the law in increasing numbers. Unfortunately, Robinson never witnessed any of her projected progress; she tragically died a year later from an overdose of medication while vacationing at her husband's family homestead in Amherst, New Hampshire.

Nevertheless, Massachusetts' first woman lawyer left an important legacy that extended beyond the professional barriers she broke in Massachusetts. Keenly aware of the dilemma of double consciousness, Robinson identified and challenged other women lawyers around the country to grapple with some of its thorniest issues, from courtroom etiquette to the dilemma of marriage and career, through her publications. These challenges endured well into the twentieth century, challenging a younger generation of women, the new women lawyers of the early twentieth century, to find solutions in the midst of an era of optimism and progress.

Portia Law School

The growth in the number of new women lawyers in the early twentieth century rested in part on Portia Law School, the first all-women's law school in the country, located in Boston. Founded in 1908 by Arthur Winfield MacLean, a graduate of Boston University School of Law, Portia was a school that provided part-time legal education to working women, mostly the daughters of Irish, Italian, and Jewish immigrants. In 1914, six years after it opened with just two students, Portia Law School boasted an enrollment of forty women, more than the total number of women who had graduated from Boston University since 1872. In 1920 alone, there were over 170 women enrolled. By 1929, nearly 30 percent of all women law students in the country were enrolled at Portia. Moreover, even as Portia grew under the shadow of the more prestigious law schools in Boston, its graduates thrived. They performed impressively on the state bar exam, scoring higher than the men who had graduated from Northeastern or Suffolk law schools throughout the 1920s. Portia Law School played a major role in accelerating the integration of a generation of women into the legal profession in the early decades of the twentieth century.

"The Golden Age of Opportunity"

By 1920, there were 1,738 women lawyers in the United States, every state bar was open to women, and most law schools admitted women. By 1930, the number of women lawyers nationwide had almost doubled, rising to 3,385. The growing numbers of women lawyers reveal the important advances women made in the legal profession in Massachusetts in the half-century from the 1880s through the 1930s.

Women in Massachusetts benefited from this era of progress. In 1905, there were enough women lawyers in the state to organize a separate, all-women's professional organization: the Massachusetts Association of Women Lawyers. In 1916, the Bar Association of the City of Boston admitted women. By 1920, the year women won the vote nationwide, Massachusetts ranked fifth among all states where women lawyers practiced, and by 1939 Massachusetts was third, behind only New York and Washington, DC.

While the late nineteenth century was an era of struggle for Robinson and other pioneer women lawyers, the 1930s, according to Massachusetts lawyer Emma Fall Schofield, was "the golden age of opportunity for women." Schofield had much to be optimistic about. The daughter of lawyers Anna Christy Fall and George Fall, Schofield followed her parents' professional path. She graduated from Boston University School of Law in 1908, married, had two children, and built a remarkable legal career. She was the first woman in Massachusetts to serve both as a commissioner on the Massachusetts Industrial Accident Board and as assistant attorney general. In addition, she was the first woman probation officer in the western part of the state, a dean of women at the Northeastern University Evening Law School, and a professor of constitutional law at Portia Law School.

In 1920, Boston lawyer Dorothy Hobson echoed Schofield's optimism, predicting that women's newly won right to vote would increase their professional opportunities even further. The impressive accomplishments of individual women throughout Massachusetts seemed to reinforce Schofield's and Hobson's buoyant confidence in the future of women in the legal profession. In 1923, Portia Law School graduate Ellen L. Buckley became the first assistant U.S. attorney in New England; in 1927, Margaret M. McChesney, another Portia graduate, became the first woman lawyer to appear before the full bench of the Massachusetts Supreme Judicial Court. Schofield herself, along with Sadie Lipner Shulman, both Boston University Law School graduates, became Massachusetts' first female judges in 1930. Both were prominent members of the bar, Schofield was the first woman assistant attorney general of Massachusetts; and Shulman was an assistant corporation counsel for the City of Boston. They were sworn in during the same ceremony: Schofield to the Malden District Court and Shulman to the Dorchester District Court.

In 1934, Ethel E. Mackiernan, a Portia graduate, was appointed to the Nantucket District Court, becoming the first woman to serve as presiding justice of a court in Massachusetts. Meanwhile, Portia graduate Blanche Braxton stood as proof that an African-American woman could also succeed in the law in this era of opportunity. In 1923, Braxton became the first African-American woman lawyer in Massachusetts, and a decade later she became the first African-American woman to practice law in the U.S. District Court in Massachusetts.

Discrimination

Despite the impressive accomplishments of individual women lawyers, most women never came close to achieving the professional status and autonomy of women like Emma Fall Schofield. Instead, a nationwide pattern of gender discrimination in the legal profession stretched from large cities like New York and Chicago, to southern cities like Baltimore and Atlanta, to cities in the west like Omaha and Tacoma. The administrator at DePaul University College of Law in Chicago attested to the pervasiveness of this gender discrimination. "Out of hundreds of requests for law clerks . . . I have never received one request for a young woman, nor have I been able to place one unless through influence, as the daughter of a lawyer." African-American women lawyers fared even worse, as race combined with gender to create even more resistance. By 1930, the U.S. Census listed only four African-American women lawyers practicing in the District of Columbia, three in New York State, and none in Massachusetts.

Women lawyers in Massachusetts did not escape this national pattern of gender discrimination in the legal profession. As early as 1912, Boston attorney Alice Parker Lesser exposed the hard reality behind women lawyers' expressions of optimism. In an interview with the *Saturday Evening Traveller*, she confessed: "I realize that for years I and other women lawyers have lied when we said that we were on an equal basis with men in our profession. It is not so, and I am going to tell the real truth about the situation now. The field of law is no better today for girls than it was 20 years ago when they entered it." Women had more opportunities than ever before to study law, Lesser acknowledged, but they still lacked the opportunity to practice it. "Of course, she has all the book learning any lawyer can have . . . but practice of law tells another tale." The title of the article in the *Saturday Evening Traveller*, "Girl Lawyer Has Small Chance for Success," summed up Lesser's gloomy picture.

Other women lawyers in Massachusetts agreed with Lesser's pessimistic view, expressing caution, if not despair, about the lack of professional opportunities available to the new women lawyers of the day. Portia

graduate Edith Batchelder explained that law was an "interesting" voca-
tion for women, but it was "not necessarily profitable." The usually optimistic Dorothy Hobson admitted that "it is much more difficult for
women to get connected with good firms than for men." The highly
trained Marjorie Hurd, who earned both a bachelor of arts and a master
of arts in economics from Radcliffe College, attended the Cambridge
Law School for Women, and then graduated from Portia Law School,
took an even dimmer view. Law "is overwhelmingly a man's profession
and in the give and take of casual and formal association a woman is at a
disadvantage," she explained. There is "very little chance for women."

Such expressions of pessimism were not misguided. In 1931, Catherine Murdock failed the oral portion of the Massachusetts bar exam when
her examiner told her that "women belong in the kitchen, not in the bar."
Finally admitted in 1932, Murdock found that no law firms would admit
women, so she joined two other Portia graduates, Elizabeth Curry and
Helen Mowles, and opened Curry, Mowles & Murdock, Boston's first
all-women's law firm. Ignoring the warnings about competing with men,
they opened their office at 6 Beacon Street and set out to practice law.
"We're just going to be ourselves. We know law and will go about it
quietly, not looking for any favors because we are women and giving the
very best advice we can." Yet, despite their claims, it was impossible for
Boston to ignore the gendered composition of Curry, Mowles & Murdock. Writing about the three women lawyers at the firm, a reporter for
the *Boston Traveler* explained that the "girls plan to cook their own
lunch. They know just as much about the culinary art as the most modern
homemaker and just between ourselves, they think law is much more
simple than making an angel food cake!"

Other women lawyers seeking work in Boston had to settle for then
gender-appropriate office positions where they assisted male lawyers.
Dorothy Hobson was a secretary and Edith Batchelder was an office
manager. With the help of Harvard professor Joseph Beale, the eminently
qualified Marjorie Hurd worked briefly as a law clerk at Hale and Dorr,
but left to become Beale's secretary. For a salary of $15 for a three-day
workweek, Hurd became the invisible assistant behind Beale's *Treatise*

on the Conflict of Laws, "looking up cases, writing the simpler chapters, revising, etc."

In addition to the challenge of finding work, women lawyers also discovered that it was very difficult to find a husband who would encourage their careers. Few new women lawyers were as fortunate as Schofield, who managed to balance marriage and motherhood with her thriving career. Instead, most discovered how difficult this was to achieve. Summing up the new realism, one new woman lawyer lamented: "Marriage is too much of a compromise; it lops off a woman's life as an individual. Yet, the renunciation too is a lopping off. We choose between the frying-pan and the fire—both very uncomfortable." Another wrote simply: "Give it up!!"

Despite the persistent obstacles, by the end of the 1930s several issues were clear. Women lawyers were practicing in every state and had established themselves as permanent members of the legal profession. Nationwide, they worked in a wide range of situations including solo practice, law firms, business offices, government agencies, and courts. These accomplishments fueled the optimism of the new women lawyers of the early twentieth century. In Boston, women could be especially optimistic about the opportunity to study law, because Portia Law School and Boston University School of Law played a crucial role in building a new generation of women lawyers for the twentieth century. In 1939 alone, thirty-one women attended Boston University Law School, while forty-nine women attended Portia, second only to New York University School of Law, where fifty-five women were enrolled. A decade later, as more law schools around the country began to admit women, the number of women studying law in Boston fell to fifty-two. Despite the drop, more than a third of all women law students in the country studied in Boston in 1949, and Massachusetts ranked fourth in the nation among all states where women practiced law in 1949.

During World War II, women made some long-sought inroads into the legal profession, finding employment opportunities in government agencies and large law firms that had long resisted hiring women. In New York City, Cadwalader became the first major Wall Street law firm to promote a woman to partner. In Washington, DC, Justice William Douglas hired the first female clerk to the Supreme Court, and the Federal Bar Association elected its first woman president. Meanwhile, in Boston, Portia graduate Catherine E. Falvey became the youngest elected member of the Massachusetts House of Representatives in 1940; joined the Armed Forces in 1942, where she became a major; and went on to become the only female department head on the American legal staff during the Nuremberg trials.

Still, patterns of discrimination persisted alongside progress. Long a city where women could gain access to legal education, the "good old conservative Boston" that Robinson described in 1888 remained resistant to women in its best law firms and closed tightly to them at the very top throughout the first half of the twentieth century. In fact, no woman became a partner in a major law firm in Boston until the 1970s.

The persistent discrimination against women lawyers in Massachusetts leaves little doubt: despite the barriers Robinson and the women of her generation broke to enter the legal profession in the Commonwealth, becoming a lawyer was just the first step in the struggle for women to rise to the top of the legal profession in Massachusetts. In addition, in the early decades of the twentieth century, as new women lawyers made additional professional inroads in Massachusetts, they still faced the thorny challenge of double consciousness. Robinson's queries about wearing a hat in court and how to balance marriage and career continued to challenge women lawyers in Massachusetts, though sometimes in different forms. It would be up to women lawyers in the latter part of the twentieth century once again to tackle the enduring dilemma of balancing their gender and professional identity.

The First Women Judges

The number of women judges in state courts in Massachusetts increased only gradually and for long stretches of time the number of women judges remained nearly constant. Between 1932 and 1972 there were never more than seven women judges in Massachusetts state courts at one time, and during each year between 1940 and 1972 there were between five and seven women judges.

It was not until the 1990s that Massachusetts saw its most significant increase in the number of women judges in state courts, from forty-one in 1990 to 102 in 2000. According to the *2010 Women in Federal and State-level Judgeships* report issued by the State University of New York at Albany's Center for Women in Government and Civil Society, Massachusetts ranked second among states for the largest share of women in state-level judgeships, with 37.5 percent (following Vermont, with 40.2 percent of state-level judgeships held by women).

While women made up 39 percent of currently sitting judges in the Massachusetts state court system and 29 percent of federal judges in the state in January 2012, those numbers lag behind the percentage of women associates at that time (45 percent) and the percentage of women law students (48 percent).

At the time Supreme Judicial Court Chief Justice Margaret H. Marshall announced her retirement in 2010, Massachusetts was one of twenty states with a woman chief justice. As this chapter is written, four of the seven justices of the Supreme Judicial Court are women. Ruth I. Abrams had, in 1978, become the first woman appointed to the Supreme Judicial Court.

As more women judges were appointed in Massachusetts, one common pattern emerged in the distribution of judges throughout the court system. Although the first two women judges were appointed to the District Court, women judges were far more common in the Probate and Family Court and Juvenile Court than in the overall court system. The first woman to sit as a judge in the Probate and Family Court, Beatrice Hancock Mullaney, was appointed in 1955. By 1978, five of the fifteen women judges in Massachusetts state courts could be found in the Probate and Family Court. Indeed, by January 2012, twenty-three of the forty-six currently sitting Probate and Family Court judges were women. This even split is eleven percentage points higher than the statewide total. The tendency of women judges to be found in the Probate and Family Court is a longstanding one in Massachusetts. In part, this is another example of Massachusetts mirroring a national trend. Women judges tend to be more concentrated in courts of limited jurisdiction and most particularly in courts such as probate and family courts because such courts consider issues more closely identified with women's traditional roles.

It was under the presidency of Jimmy Carter, when the first significant increase in the number of women federal judges occurred, that some interesting differences between the numbers of women judges in the state and federal systems emerged. During his term in office, President Carter appointed forty women to the federal judiciary (including Rya W. Zobel, the first woman federal judge in Massachusetts), a significant increase above the six women federal judges who were serving at the start of his presidency. Commentators have attributed this increase to several factors, including the passage of the 1978 Omnibus Judgeship Act, which created 152 new judicial seats, as well as President Carter's adoption of a merit selection plan for judicial appointments and an explicit outreach policy intended to increase the number of women appointees. In the Massachusetts state courts, with no increase in the number of judicial positions such as occurred in the federal judiciary and no explicit outreach program in place, the number of women judges increased much more gradually. During the same period of President Carter's administration, for example, the number of women judges in Massachusetts state courts grew only slightly, increasing from thirteen in 1977 to nineteen in 1981.

In Massachusetts, the role of institutional advocate for appointing more women came initially from women lawyers' organizations. Both the Women's Bar Association of Massachusetts and the Massachusetts Association of Women Lawyers put the appointment of women judges at the top of their priority lists starting in the late 1970s. Their advocacy— meeting with the governor, running workshops for women interested in becoming judges, compiling directories of interested women for the appointing authorities, later holding seats on the Judicial Nominating Commission—was instrumental in providing a voice and a resource on this issue. This is consistent with the advocacy and support role of other comparable women's organizations, such as the National Association of Women Judges, founded in 1979. This advocacy undoubtedly was a factor in the substantial increases in the number of women judges starting around 1980. According to the American Bar Association, the proportion of women judges nationally doubled between 1980 and 1991, and in Massachusetts the number of women judges during the same period increased from seventeen to forty-four.

Conclusion

The history of women lawyers and judges provides an important backdrop for those who practice, and judge, today in Massachusetts. In over 130 years, there has been much progress. Women have achieved positions of power and influence in the legal profession, to an extent unimaginable by Lelia J. Robinson. Yet, while certain barriers faced by the first women lawyers no longer exist, there is still work to be done to achieve true parity in all professional settings of the law. If past is prologue, our sisters in law will continue to make incremental progress on that front for some time.

Biographies of Selected Pioneering Massachusetts Women Lawyers

Anna Christy Fall
1855–1930, admitted 1891
First woman to argue before a jury in Massachusetts

Anna Christy Fall pushed to increase legal rights for all women.[3] Born in Chelsea, Massachusetts, in 1855, Fall worked as a typesetter before enrolling at Boston University to study journalism. At BU, she met her husband, George Howard Fall, who established his own legal practice. Fall was integral in her husband's practice, working in his office and sitting beside him in court to assist him as his hearing worsened. Through her work, Fall developed her own strong interest in the law and, while raising three small children, enrolled in Boston University School of Law in 1889. She took the December 1890 Massachusetts bar exam and was admitted in January 1891. Fall graduated magna cum laude from BU Law in June 1891 and began practicing with her husband under the firm name Fall & Fall. The couple practiced together for forty years.

Many early women lawyers delegated courtroom matters to their husbands, but Fall chose to become an active trial lawyer. In November 1891, only five months after her graduation, she became the first woman in Massachusetts to argue a case before a jury, winning $700 for her client.

In addition to her practice, Fall took an active role in the women's suffrage movement. Speaking alongside prominent suffragist Lucy Stone, Fall advocated around the state for equal rights for women. She also sought to change discriminatory laws. Her book, *The Tragedy of a Widow's Third*, published in 1898, was distributed to every member of the Massachusetts House and Senate and was a key force in helping pass the 1902 legislation that eliminated the practice of the "widow's third." She also advocated for equal guardianship rights for mothers, which became law in 1902. Fall lectured, wrote, and practiced law until her death in 1930.

Emma Fall Schofield
1885–1980, admitted 1908
First woman judge in Massachusetts (with Sadie Lipner Shulman)

Emma Fall Schofield built upon the accomplishments of her mother, Anna Christy Fall, and others in the women's rights movement to become one of the first two female judges in Massachusetts. Schofield, born in Malden, Massachusetts, earned her bachelor of arts from Boston University in 1906 and her bachelor of laws from BU Law just two years later. Following graduation, she studied law at the Sorbonne and Paris Law School for one year before joining her parents' firm, Fall & Fall.

In a time when only around fifty women actively practiced law in Massachusetts (most reading law in the confines of a relative's office), Schofield's legal endeavors were groundbreaking. Schofield founded the Malden Women's Equal Suffrage League and campaigned for suffrage across the state. In 1922, at age thirty-seven, she was appointed by Governor Channing Cox as commissioner of the Massachusetts Industrial Accident Board, a quasi-judicial position she held for five years. Then, only seven years after women obtained the right to vote, Schofield was named the first woman assistant attorney general in Massachusetts in 1927.

In 1930, Governor Frank Allen simultaneously appointed Schofield to the Malden District Court and Sadie Lipner Shulman to the Dorchester District Court. Schofield would serve in that position for twenty-seven years until her retirement in 1957. During her years on the bench, she taught classes at Portia Law School and the Chandler School of Boston while lecturing to the general public on topics including everyday law for women and wit and wisdom of the bench and bar.

Throughout her life, Schofield worked to assist probationers and juvenile delinquents. In addition to her law degree, Schofield received a degree in 1911 from the Boston School of Social Workers. She was the first female probation officer in the Springfield District Court. Later in her career, Schofield studied the prevention of juvenile delinquency around the country, citing a lack of moral training and discipline as its chief cause.

Among her many accomplishments, Schofield was president of the Professional Women's Club of Boston, the Women Graduates' Club of Boston University, the Woman's Republican Club of Malden, and the Business and Professional Women's Republican Club of Massachusetts. In addition to being a member of the American Bar Association, she was the first woman elected to its local council in Massachusetts. In the last decade of her life, Schofield authored three books about her parents and childhood, including *Anna Christy Fall, My Remarkable Mother.*

Elizabeth Marston
1893–1993, admitted 1918
The inspiration for Wonder Woman

Children and adults have adored superheroes for decades, but few know that a woman lawyer inspired the creation of Wonder Woman.[4] When William Moulton Marston, a psychologist, decided to create a new superhero, his wife Elizabeth urged him to make the superhero a woman. She reportedly said, "We have enough male superheroes already. Let's have a female superhero!" William agreed and modeled his new superhero after his wife. Wonder Woman, a strong and wise warrior, bore marked similarities to Elizabeth Marston. Marston received a B.A. in psychology from Mount Holyoke College in 1915 and continued her studies at Boston University School of Law. When she asked her parents for BU's $100 tuition fee, Marston was told she belonged at home, not in the public sphere, so she sold cookbooks to raise the money. She was one of three women in BU Law's 1918 graduating class.

After she was admitted to the Massachusetts bar Marston joined her husband in Harvard's psychology labs. Together they worked to develop the polygraph lie detector test while William earned a Ph.D. and Elizabeth a master's degree. Their work inspired the magic Lasso of Truth.

Marston worked with astounding energy to support her family and further her career. She lectured on law, ethics, and psychology at New York University and American University; served as an editor of *Encyclopedia Britannica*; and indexed the documents of the first fourteen Congresses. During the Great Depression, Marston kept her family fed as assistant to the chief executive of Metropolitan Life Insurance. When her husband created Wonder Woman in 1941, Marston's strength and resilience in the male-dominated public realm made her the perfect model for the wise and caring crusading superhero. Wonder Woman made her debut in *All Star Comics* in December 1941, published under William Marston's pen name Charles Moulton, and to this day remains one of the most popular comic-book characters.

Sadie Lipner Shulman
1891–1998, admitted 1912
First woman judge in Massachusetts (with Emma Fall Schofield)

Sadie Lipner Shulman was inspired to become a lawyer when she met her uncle, a lawyer in Poland, as a child.[5] Although she lived in a country where women were not yet able to vote, she pursued her dream and became one of the most legally accomplished women of her time.

Shulman was born in New York City in 1891. Her family moved to Boston, where she graduated from Roxbury High School and then enrolled in Boston University School of Law in 1908. At age seventeen Shulman was the youngest member of her class, and when she graduated at age twenty, she did not meet the age requirements for admission to the

Massachusetts bar. She was admitted a year later, in 1912. By 1913 she had been named chief counsel for the Boston Civic Service. She married Charles Shulman, a prominent Boston attorney, and in 1918 they established the firm Shulman and Shulman. The couple had one son.

During her early legal career, Shulman focused on trial practice, specializing in domestic issues such as adoption and divorce. In 1926 she was appointed assistant corporation counsel for the City of Boston; she was the first woman to hold the position.

By 1930 Governor Frank Allen decided it was time for women to be represented in the judicial branch in Massachusetts. Recognizing her accomplishments and ability, the governor named Shulman special justice to the Dorchester District Court (while simultaneously appointing Emma Fall Schofield special justice to the Malden District Court). The appointments made her and Schofield the state's first woman judges, and made Shulman the first Jewish woman judge in the state. In one notable case, Shulman sentenced a juvenile who had killed a pedestrian while driving a stolen car to go view the victim's body at the funeral home. She observed, "I believe that if there is anything you can show a person in reality that will help them or prevent them from repeating a wrong, then it should be done."

Shulman served on the court until 1973, when a Constitutional amendment was passed by the voters instituting a mandatory retirement age of seventy for Massachusetts' judges.

In addition to her judicial accomplishments, Shulman was president of the Massachusetts Association of Women Lawyers, founded and served as the first president of the Business and Professional Women's Republican Club of Massachusetts, served as a Republican presidential elector, and was the first female president of the Boston University School of Law Alumni Association. Shulman died at age 107.

Inez C. Fields
1896–1978, admitted 1924
First African-American woman to graduate from Boston University Law School

Inez C. Fields was born in Hampton, Virginia, in 1896.[6] As an African American in Virginia, Fields had difficulty gaining a proper education in the public schools. Seeking better educational opportunities, Fields and her family moved to Massachusetts, where she graduated from Cambridge High School in 1918. Still excluded from Virginia law schools due to her race, Fields enrolled at Boston University School of Law. Although the school had admitted women and African-American students for several years, Fields became the first African-American woman to graduate from the school in 1922.

Two years later, in 1924, Fields became the second African-American woman admitted to the bar in Massachusetts. (The first African-American woman, Blanche E. Braxton, had been admitted in 1923.) She returned to Virginia, where she became that state's third African-American woman admitted to the bar in 1928. She joined her father, George Washington Fields, in his practice. She died in 1978.

Timeline of Notable Firsts

First	Who	When
Lawyer in Massachusetts	Lelia J. Robinson	1882
Assistant U.S. attorney	Ellen L. Buckley	1923
Woman to argue before full bench of the Supreme Judicial Court	Margaret M. McChesney	1927
Judges in Massachusetts (District Court)	Hon. Emma Fall Schofield Hon. Sadie Lipner Shulman	1930
All-woman law firm	Curry, Mowles and Murdock	1932
Presiding justice of a Massachusetts court (Nantucket District Court)	Ethel E. Mackiernan	1934
Dean of a Massachusetts law school (Portia Law School)	Margaret H. Bauer	1952
Partner of a large Boston law firm (Palmer & Dodge)	Virginia H. Aldrich	1969
Chief justice of a Massachusetts state court (Land Court)	Hon. Marilyn M. Sullivan	1973
Associate justice, Supreme Judicial Court	Hon. Ruth I. Abrams	1978
Judge, U.S. District Court for the District of Massachusetts	Hon. Rya W. Zobel	1979
U.S. magistrate judge (in Massachusetts)	Hon. Joyce London Alexander	1979

First	Who	When
President, Massachusetts Bar Association	Alice E. Richmond	1986
President, Boston Bar Association	Gene D. Dahmen	1987
President, Massachusetts Continuing Legal Education	Mary E. Weber	1990
District attorney	Elizabeth D. Scheibel	1993
Judge, First Circuit	Hon. Sandra L. Lynch	1995
Managing partner of one of Boston's largest law firms (Goodwin Procter & Hoar LLP)	Regina M. Pisa	1998
Chief justice, Supreme Judicial Court	Hon. Margaret H. Marshall	1999
Elected to statewide office (Massachusetts state treasurer)	Shannon O'Brien	1999
Sheriff	Andrea Cabral	2002
Massachusetts attorney general	Martha Coakley	2006
Bar counsel, Office of the Bar Counsel	Constance V. Vecchione	2007
U.S. attorney for the district of Massachusetts	Carmen M. Ortiz	2009
Massachusetts state auditor	Suzanne M. Bump	2011
U.S. senator for Massachusetts	Elizabeth Warren	2013

Endnotes

[1] For information on supporting sources, see that original publication.

[2] *Lelia J. Robinson's Case*, 131 Mass. 376 (1881).

[3] The information presented on Anna Christy Fall is derived from Frances E. Willard & Mary A. Livermore, eds., *A Woman of the Century, Fourteen-Hundred Seventy Biographical Sketches Accompanied by Portraits of Leading American Women*, 283–84 (Moulton 1893).

[4] The information presented on Elizabeth Marston is derived from: "Wonder Woman: a MoHo?" *The Mount Holyoke News*, Mar. 10, 2006, *available at* http://themhnews.org/2006/03/features/wonder-woman-a-moho; Marguerite Lamb, "Who Was Wonder Woman?," *Bostonia*, Fall 2001, *available at* http://www.bu.edu/bostonia/fall01/woman; Phone Interview with Moulton "Pete" Marston (Apr. 20, 2012).

[5] The information presented on Sadie Lipner Shulman is derived from: John R. Vile, ed., *Great American Judges: An Encyclopedia* (ABC-CLIO, Inc. 2003); "First Woman Judges Named in Baystate," *Boston Daily Globe*, Dec. 11, 1930; *Bostonia*, Summer 1960; "Panel Recognizes Astral Advances in Women in Law," *BU Bridge*, Apr. 19, 2002; "World News About Women," *The Women's Journal*, Jan. 1931; "Sadie Lipner Shulman," *Woman's Lawyers Journal*, Aug. 1932, at 23; "Jewess Named Justice by Massachusetts Governor," *Jewish Telegraphic Agency*, Dec. 12, 1930.

[6] The information presented on Inez C. Fields is derived from: J. Clay Smith, Jr., *Emancipation: The Making of the Black Lawyer* 1844–1944, 111, 232, 237 (Univ. of Penn. Press 1993) (citing Feb. 22, 1991 letter of Richard J. Rouse, Clerk of the Supreme Judicial Court for Suffolk County, verifying Fields' admission date as Apr. 15, 1924).

CHAPTER

V

The Experience of LGBT Lawyers

Joyce Kauffman, Esq.
John Ward, Esq.

The Early Years: Survival and Beyond

In 1970, it was unthinkable for an openly LGBT lawyer to practice in Massachusetts. Same-sex relations were "the abominable and detestable crime against nature" (G.L. c. 272, § 34, which is still on the books), and LGBT people were considered to be diseased or morally tainted. Today, without concealing our sexual identities, we are partners in prestigious law firms, professors in law schools, judges, and successful practitioners in small or solo firms. In other words, we are thoroughly integrated into the profession at every level. How did this happen, and how did it happen so remarkably quickly? Some of the answers remain mysterious, but some of it is the result of acts of courage and decency on the part of ourselves, the sense of justice of the courts and legislative and administrative bodies we serve in, and the social tolerance of our fellow citizens in the Commonwealth, which shines forth in surprising ways and at unexpected times. What follows are some individual stories. Choosing some stories inevitably means leaving out others, equally significant. We wish this were not the case, and we offer our sincere regrets to the many, many brave pioneers whose individual stories are not part of this brief sampling.

For some of us, coming out as LGBT lawyers back in the 1970s was a personal necessity; there was simply no other acceptable way to go. That's how it was for Katherine Triantafillou, the first openly lesbian lawyer in the Commonwealth. Steeped in feminism and inspired by feminist lawyers like Nancy Gertner, Katherine's way of coming out was simply to start representing LGBT clients and making no bones about her own sexual identity. Although she characteristically downplays her role, what she did was not only brave, but trailblazing. It is easy to forget that in the 1970s and 1980s harassment of persons identified as LGBT was common. Mary Bonauto recalls regularly running the gauntlet to taunts and curses as she left her Jamaica Plain home to go to classes at Northeastern University School of Law. For Katherine, the early years were a mix of subtle and not-so-subtle discrimination, but also support and encouragement, sometimes from surprising and unexpected places. Some lesbians warned her against coming out; others joined her, forming the Lesbian Lawyers and Legal Workers Group. Looking back, Katherine recalls that the first ten years were the most difficult. It was often hard to be taken seriously and respectfully as a professional, for people to see beyond sexual or gender orientation. For instance, Ben Klein, a lawyer at Gay & Lesbian Advocates & Defenders (GLAD), recalls a prospective employer assuring him that the firm was "neutral as to personal eccentricities." As Katherine puts it, "you had to be three times as good as a non-LGBT lawyer." Slowly, things got better. By the mid-1980s, and certainly after the passage of the law forbidding discrimination on the basis of sexual orientation in 1989, Katherine began to feel like a lawyer who happened to be a lesbian, rather than "that lesbian lawyer." She continues to represent lesbian and gay clients in a variety of contexts, as well as other individuals who are victims of discrimination and abuse as part of a small, progressive Boston firm.

Gary Buseck began the process of coming out while he was still a Jesuit seminarian in the late 1970s. The process led him to leave the Jesuits on amicable, mutually respectful terms and enroll at Boston College Law School. He and a lesbian friend felt quite isolated at BC Law because, as was common at law schools in those years (with the exception of Northeastern University School of Law), the idea of an LGBT law students association was inconceivable. However, once he was admitted, Gary's experience as an openly gay lawyer was a good one. He teamed up with Steve Ansolabehere, a good lawyer and a very good man taken from us too early by AIDS, and they began a community service oriented law practice at Two Park Square in Boston, down the hall from John Ward. Gary worked part-time at a Boston firm, Parker, Coulter, Daley & White, to supplement the meager fees that were standard for LGBT lawyers in those years. Eventually, after a fire in their offices in Park Square, Gary moved full-time to Parker, Coulter. He remembers the experience as supportive. His colleagues valued his formidable legal skills and accepted him for who he was. While at Parker, Coulter, Gary continued his involvement in lesbian and gay cases, in 1989 most famously playing a significant part in a lawsuit brought by proponents of putting a referendum on the state ballot to repeal the recently enacted sexual orientation nondiscrimination bill. The referendum proponents sued the attorney general, who was refusing to certify the ballot question. Gary represented members of the state legislature who intervened in the lawsuit in opposition to the referendum. Ultimately, the Supreme Judicial Court agreed with the attorney general's decision to refuse to certify the referendum for the ballot. Gary's firm paid the substantial costs of litigation as part of Gary's legitimate pro bono work. Afterward, Gary found his way to employment at GLAD. Except for a brief stint at Lambda Legal

Defense in New York, Gary has been with GLAD ever since. He has earned the respect of his colleagues, of all shades of the sexual orientation and gender identity spectrum, for the high quality of his legal work and his outstanding personal integrity.

Another Jesuit seminarian turned activist lawyer is Richard Iandoli. Like Gary, Richard's commitment to social justice is passionate and deep-rooted. Unlike many of the people whose stories are told in this chapter, Richard is a native of the Commonwealth. He comes from a large, first-generation Italian-American family that settled in Worcester. Family ties, as well as the climate of discrimination against LGBT people, were a consideration in Richard's coming out as a gay lawyer after he graduated from Northeastern University School of Law in 1976. In addition, Richard was concerned about the effect that making his own sexual orientation public would have on his clients, many of whom were already disadvantaged. Richard talks about feeling like an outsider and, from the beginning, many of his clients were racial and ethnic minorities, as well as LGBT people, many of them closeted, most of them not wealthy or connected. If reticence about being open concerning his sexual identity was a factor in Richard's professional life, there was no such hesitation in stepping up to represent unpopular causes and disfavored individuals. This passion for justice and equality led him to focus more and more on immigration work, where openness about his orientation would be doubly dangerous, since homosexuality was labeled sexual psychopathy and until 1990 was grounds for exclusion. Richard's identification with unpopular causes and people got him "fag-baited" even before he was totally open about his own orientation, because it is not uncommon for lawyers who represent society's rejects to be to some extent rejected themselves, whether the clients are Haitian refugees or persons accused of consensual sex with teenagers. People like Richard make real our profession's commitment to represent people who need representation, without regard to their wealth or respectability. His willingness to put himself forward in this way has been a significant factor in bringing about social change and has, over time, made it easier for Richard to be a highly successful and respected immigration lawyer and man happily married to another man.

For Cindy Rizzo, who practiced law in Boston in the 1980s, coming out was a matter of just not wanting to carry the burden of being closeted any longer. As a law student she had serious concerns that her ability to practice law would be jeopardized by her volunteer work for *Gay Community News*, which played a crucial role in creating and shaping our identity as LGBT people. Despite her fears, Cindy decided she'd had enough of being closeted and she said so, emphatically and publicly in an op-ed that was published in *GCN*.

John Ward also used *GCN* as his way of coming out as a lawyer. After clerking for a wonderful federal judge who "didn't really get it, but was supportive anyhow," John went into private practice in Boston in 1977 and shortly thereafter placed an advertisement in *GCN* announcing that his firm was "serving the community." The results were immediate. One of John's first cases was a suit against the Suffolk County district attorney, seeking to enjoin him from maintaining a hotline for the public to report "suspicious activities involving men and boys." John remembers about that case that he was terrified of going to court (partly because opposing counsel called him "honey"). John got Michael Avery, a straight colleague, to go to court with him, and the district attorney's office agreed to discontinue the hotline. The furor continued, however, when the group that hired John held a fundraiser at the Arlington Street Church to pay his fee. The speaker was Gore Vidal and in attendance was the then–chief justice of the Superior Court, Robert Bonin, who wanted to hear Vidal, the historian. That the program was a fundraiser for the defense in a case pending before the Superior Court led to a proceeding in the Supreme Judicial Court that in turn would ultimately lead to Bonin's resignation. John was subpoenaed as a witness. Nancy Gertner represented him (for no fee) and John was not called. As John recalls, the experience drove home the lesson that "being a gay lawyer was not going to be a day at the beach."

Shortly after the Bonin affair, the Boston police began arresting men en masse for allegedly engaging in sexual behavior in the Boston Public

Library. The community's reaction was immediate and loud. Gay men and some of their lesbian allies organized a picket line in front of the library. Along with a number of other lawyers, John defended the men in criminal court and spoke out publicly against what he saw as a pattern of selective enforcement targeting gay men, not only in Boston but throughout the state. Sensing that the time was right, he and a few other nonlawyer activists created a public interest law firm, GLAD, or, as it was more soberly styled (in response to a pervasive climate of fear), "Park Square Advocates." GLAD began as a vehicle for John to do pro bono cases and other legal work for individuals and groups whose legal issues involved matters of concern to the larger community. In addition, from the beginning there was an educational and consciousness-raising aspect to GLAD. Invitations for John to speak were frequent and John accepted them all, spreading the word that LGBT people had rights, and that there was a group that would assist in their struggles. Nevertheless, there was a real question in the early days as to whether GLAD would morph from what seemed like a really good idea into a community organization with roots and permanence. A pivotal moment came in the spring of 1980, when John got a call from John Gaffney, who was active in the Rhode Island chapter of the American Civil Liberties Union (ACLU). Mr. Gaffney had been approached by Aaron Fricke, an eighteen-year-old high school senior at Cumberland High School. Aaron wanted to attend the senior prom with a male date, Paul Guilbert, another eighteen-year-old. He had been turned down by the principal of the school and the school board. It was time to go to court, and John, with the help of a great Rhode Island attorney, Lynette Labinger, filed suit in federal court in Providence. Aaron was a wonderful witness, and the team succeeded in obtaining an injunction from federal judge Raymond J. Pettine requiring the school to let Aaron and Paul dance with their fellow seniors. The publicity was enormous, and Aaron, as a result of his television appearances, began receiving letters from lesbian and gay teenagers from all over the country, kids who had thought they were all alone.

For GLAD, the Fricke case provided much-needed reassurance that the organization was here to stay. That summer, Jose Gomez, a Harvard law student, came on board to supplement John's meager administrative skills and to begin the nuts-and-bolts work of creating a grassroots membership organization and raising money. The momentum was there, and by the time Kevin Cathcart, a young lawyer from Northeastern Law School, began his tenure as executive director, GLAD was emerging as a recognized force in the struggle for LGBT rights in Massachusetts. John left Boston in 1983, to do death penalty work in California. As he says, "It was time to give GLAD some space and room to grow and become what it was meant to be. Founder energy and sustainer energy are very different. I was given the grace to realize that I had the former, but not the latter." Notwithstanding, John felt the pull and returned to Boston and to GLAD for a few years in the 1990s. Inevitably, he was drawn into the struggle and, among other activities, he represented a group of Irish-American lesbians and gay men as they (unsuccessfully) took their fight to be included in the annual South Boston St. Patrick's Day Parade to the U.S. Supreme Court. Although they lost, John remembers the duel with multiple opponents with pleasure and especially savors the fact that he was the first openly gay man to appear before and argue a case decided by the Supreme Court.[1]

GLAD did indeed grow in John's absence, "beyond my wildest dreams," he says. The 1980s were a tumultuous decade for GLAD, remembered mostly for a sometimes bitter (but ultimately victorious) struggle over LGBT foster parents and by Gary Buseck's successful effort to retain the Massachusetts statute offering protection against discrimination based on sexual orientation (and, more recently, gender identity).

In 1990, GLAD took a quantum leap forward when Mary Bonauto became civil rights director, having come to Boston from Maine, where she had been one of three openly gay or lesbian lawyers in the state. Mary's work on behalf of the LGBT community over the decades flows naturally from her innate sense of fairness and justice, an inner strength that moved her forward in the face of massive opposition, including verbal and physical harassment. There is no argument that Mary has been an indispensable actor in the legal and educational process that has made marriage for same-sex couples a reality in many states, beginning with Massachusetts. It is not hyperbole to call her "our Thurgood Marshall."

GLAD has since grown in other ways as well. GLAD was one of the first responders to the AIDS catastrophe, lending legal support from the early 1980s onward to the massive community effort to provide support and care for those stricken, regardless of their sexual orientation or identity. This effort became exponentially more focused when GLAD hired Ben Klein as director of the AIDS Law Project in 1994. Ben was "out" as a teenager and active in BAGLY (Boston Area Gay and Lesbian Youth). Significantly, in terms of the situation of LGBT lawyers, he felt it necessary to pull back a bit when he went to law school, where he faced his share of ostracism when he came out as a gay lawyer. Ben agrees that times have changed, but he is keenly aware that change is uneven and that, except in a few rarified milieus, it is still not possible for a young LGBT person to have a normal adolescence. He works to change that.

If truth be told, parts of "LGB" community have not always been enthusiastic or comfortable embracing the "T" community. GLAD has always fought against that discomfort. Hence, it was no surprise when, in 1998, GLAD hired Jennifer Levi, a lesbian-identified transgender person (she is currently director of GLAD's Transgender Rights Project, formally created in 2008). A brilliant lawyer and a former law clerk to Judge Michael Boudin on the First Circuit, Jennifer has no illusions about the magnitude of her task nor the glacial pace of change, but her commitment to equality and social change is unstoppable, just like that of the other lawyers and workers at GLAD.

GLAD's story is inspiring and a catalyst for much of what has happened for LGBT lawyers in Massachusetts. But it is, after all, just one story among many. Here are some of the others.

Individual Lawyers' Experiences

Selected Reflections and Interviews
Presented by year admitted to the bar.

Hon. Dermot Meagher
Admitted 1966

(*Originally written in 2008 by Hon. Dermot Meagher and entitled:* How I Became the First (Openly) Gay Judge in Massachusetts. *It has been edited for this publication.*)

My academic qualifications were not an issue. I graduated from Harvard College in 1962, Boston College Law School in 1965, had been a fellow at the Harvard Center for Criminal Justice at Harvard Law School. I also had the professional qualifications, but so did a lot of other lawyers in Massachusetts. My resumé was eclectic, but interesting. I had been an assistant district attorney, in private practice, a bail reformer, a court reformer, and an investigator and prosecutor of lawyers.

In 1981, still at my job investigating and prosecuting lawyers for the Supreme Judicial Court of Massachusetts, I began studies at the Kennedy School of Government at Harvard in their mid-career Masters in Public Administration program. It was a wonderful experience. I took courses I had avoided in college, like economics, and a brilliant government course with the unlikely name "Bureaucracy," taught by James Q. Wilson. It was the hardest course I ever studied.

The most fortuitous course I enrolled in, at least for my future career, was taught by Michael S. Dukakis, who had been defeated for reelection as governor of Massachusetts in 1980 after one term. I almost did not take the course because I thought he had been too spartan, rigid, and unpolitical as governor in his first term. A wiser friend of mine, Tom Vallely, then a Massachusetts state representative, said, "Are you a fool? This man ran the state for four years. He did a great job. He may run it again. He is one of the best teachers here."

Tom Vallely was correct.

Even as governor, Michael Dukakis was famous for riding on public transportation, "the T" as we call it. Sometimes on my way to school on the Red Line from Charles Station to Harvard Square, if he nodded recognition in response to my stare, I would talk to him on his last leg to Cambridge from Brookline.

Contrary to his public image, he was very amiable, listened to people, and engaged his audience. He was also kind and not at all interested in putting anyone down. (It may have been his thick eyebrows that made him appear fiercer than he really was.) Most of us in this mid-career program had been away from school for a while, and we were not always the most articulate. His course was entitled "The External Management of a Public Agency." In other words, the course was about how to get along with the outside world—the media, the legislature, the executive (a mayor, governor, or president), and the public. It was a very good course, taught by examples, the case method, just like they do at Harvard Business School. The governor gave me an "A."

I was "out" as a recovering alcoholic in my office, and even to the dean of admissions at the Kennedy School, but I still was not "out" as a gay man. Then, in the early 1980s a friend, John Ward, one of the first openly gay lawyers in Massachusetts, certainly the lawyer who was most "out" and out-front fighting homophobic laws and governmental practices, asked me to serve on the litigation committee of GLAD, an organization he had founded to handle cases that deal with issues larger than those faced by the litigants themselves. I was very nervous about it, but knew that my new boss sat on a board of the Civil Liberties Union of Massachusetts (CLUM). I hoped that he would be understanding.

One day on the way to lunch, I asked my boss if he was on CLUM's litigation committee. He replied that he was not, but that he was on CLUM's board of directors. He then said, "Why do you ask?"

"Because I've been asked to be on the litigation committee of GLAD."

"What's GLAD?" he asked.

"It's the Gay and Lesbian Advocates and Defenders, kind of a civil liberties union specifically for gay issues. John Ward founded it."

After a pause my boss said, "I don't think you should be on that committee."

I said, "OK." I did not ask the reason. It may well have been because as a person who was investigating and prosecuting lawyers I should not be on any committee that chose lawyers to work on cases. It may have been something else. Frankly, I was relieved by my boss's response. John Ward had challenged me to be "out" beyond my courage at that time. When I reported the conversation to John he said, "Well then, we'll put you on the board of directors of GLAD. If he can be on the Civil Liberties Union board of directors, you can be on the GLAD board of directors." So, there I was. I had no response; John had me. Today I am ashamed to say that at first I wanted to be an anonymous board member, but I got over that quickly.

Also in the early 1980s it became apparent to me and some other gay and lesbian lawyers that we would never gain the attention of the organized bar, the administration of the courts, the Supreme Judicial Court, the governor, or anyone else until we were organized. There were already a number of minority bar associations. These associations, even the smallest of them, had influence. They were routinely consulted by the Supreme Judicial Court, the governor, and the legal establishment on a number of topics, changes in court rules and the appointment of judges being two important ones. So we organized.

At first the gay men and the lesbians met separately, but eventually in 1985 three women, Sandy Smales, Katherine Triantafillou, and Cindy Rizzo, and three male lawyers, Vincent ("Vin") McCarthy, Richard Burns, and I, got together and created the Massachusetts Lesbian and Gay Bar Association (MLGBA). It is now the second-largest minority bar association in Massachusetts.

In 1983, after graduating from the Kennedy School, I decided to apply to become a judge. It seemed to me that the only court that could pretend to any sort of cosmopolitanism sufficient to tolerate a gay member was the Boston Municipal Court. The first African-American chief justice, the first African-American woman judge, and the first Latino judge had been appointed to that court up to that point.

There was, and still is, a lengthy, searching questionnaire/application which, to my mind, required me to "come out." It asked numerous questions about public service activity and organizations. Most of my organizations involved gay people or people in recovery. It also had an "Eagleton" question: "Is there anything in your background which would be embarrassing to the Governor, or which could unfairly be so interpreted by others?"

Before I submitted this application, a friend of mine, who was very well connected to the recently reelected Governor Dukakis, called me out of the blue. He said, "You're on a list of 100 people to be appointed to a job by the governor. I've arranged a meeting for you with the governor. Don't tell him you're gay." The following is based on my notes, made as soon as I got home after the interview.

On September 28, 1983 at ten to four I arrived at the governor's office and announced myself to the lady sitting at the front desk. I sat on the couch opposite the portraits of Governors Paul Dever, Christian Herter, and Robert Bradford. I sought courage from Paul Dever. He had appointed my father to a judgeship thirty-two years earlier and he was a bachelor too. If my father, why not me, I thought, disbelieving. I got up, sat down, got up again, signed the guestbook for posterity, and then was led to a chamber closer to the corner office. I found myself next to an aide who recognized my name and knew my younger brother and the rest of it, but not the all of it.

His Excellency came out of the door to the left, shorter than I remembered, without his jacket, and angry, or so it appeared.

I was told by the governor to sit at a table. I didn't know which chair to choose and simultaneously thought of the message of the parable, "the last shall be first," and contemporary self-help books. "the first shall be first."

I sat at the middle of the table.

Meanwhile, the governor heatedly discussed legislation with the aide. I was flattered that he let me listen in.

All of a sudden he pulled a chair around in front of me and said, "You look wonderful. Sorry about this delay. I was away all day and although it's fun to be out of here, it's hard to catch up."

I said, "It was good to watch you. It was a lot like being in your class again." Thinking that somebody ought to get down to business, I continued, "I've made efforts to join your administration since before the inauguration." I had half-heartedly applied for some regulatory jobs.

He noted my salary on a pad he held in his hand and said, "High for public service." He then said how eager he was to have me join his administration.

I replied, "This summer my father retired as a judge. So, I filled out an application for the Boston Municipal Court, but I heard that the two vacancies were committed."

He grimaced at that. Judgeships were not supposed to be "committed" to anyone in this very process-oriented administration. He said, "Not necessarily. You shouldn't limit yourself to that court."

I said, "Well, I thought that it was appropriate because I live in the district." (In Governor Dukakis' first term, judges were required to live in the district in which they served.)

"You don't have to live in the district. You know we have judges going everywhere these days."

"I know, but I also thought that it was appropriate because I'm gay, as you may know, and the Boston Municipal Court district is 25 to 35 percent gay." That was the estimate of Tommy Vallely, the district's state representative.

I didn't believe I'd said it until he said, "You know, some people are urging me to do affirmative action for gay people. I don't buy it. I just can't see it."

His intonation seemed to call for a response. "I'm not asking for affirmative action. I'm asking for representation. Although many of the defendants in that court are black, there are probably more gay people than black people in the district, probably more gay men than blacks. Gay people are the single largest minority in the district and there are gay cases up there. I saw three cases involving gay people when I was at the court the other day. One was obvious, transvestites hooking in Park Square."

He nodded sagely.

I added, "But the others weren't so obvious. I knew the defendants to be gay because of the situations and because I'd recognized one of the complainants from around town. It was a lovers' fight and one guy wanted to withdraw the assault and battery with a dangerous weapon and robbery charges against the man with whom he'd lived for five years."

The governor said, "You know, for those of us who aren't gay it's difficult to think of affirmative action for gay people. I'm sure that I've appointed gay people." Then there was a pause. He didn't name anybody, and, as far as I knew (and I and my friends had looked), there was nobody who was out of the closet in his administration. "I just wish we could be neutral on the subject," he added.

"Me too," I said.

"I don't think it should be a plus. It used to be a minus," he said, as if that should be news to me.

"I know. I'm not here as 'the gay candidate.' For one thing, gay people don't have a candidate. The gay community is as diverse as any other. But I bring it up because your application seems to call for a declaration that I'm gay."

"Where?" he asked. He seemed surprised.

I took the application out and read from it: "Is there anything in your background which would reflect adversely on the Governor or which could be unfairly so interpreted by others?"

There was a pause. Then he said, "I'm angry that people think I'd be embarrassed if someone told me that they were gay."

"Well, that's what it asks, and I didn't fill this application out lightly. I talked to a lot of people about how to deal with this issue. Some said I should say it. Others said no. But I wouldn't want to be a judge without you knowing that I am gay. I am what I am. You know that it's a dilemma for us to come out or not. We can hide with all the psychological damage that brings, or if we come out, we're thought to be militants. It's hard to be neutral on the subject. Besides that, if I didn't tell you I'm gay, it makes me just one more Irish Catholic guy applying for a job where they are already a surplus. And that's unfair because I'm not exactly welcome in those circles by reason of being gay. I talked to your legal counsel and he thought that 'being gay' was just the kind of information the question sought to elicit. I'll answer the question any way you want, but the fact that I'm gay will be apparent in the answers to the questions about my community and professional service. Most of mine is with gay people, in gay causes, or with alcoholics. I'm a recovering alcoholic as well." I might as well go for broke, I thought.

"Did you say that, too?" the governor asked.

"Yes, there's a question that asks, 'Have you ever been treated for alcoholism?' I was never specifically treated for alcoholism but I am an alcoholic. I've been sober eight and a half years."

At the door he said again how eager he was to have me in the administration and talked of a regulatory commission. "You're a very talented man. It may not be today or tomorrow. It may be next week or a few months. My legal counsel will be in touch with you."

I thanked him very much and was out the door, certain he would not hire me soon, but I appreciated his candor. He could have avoided the whole discussion. I do not think that anyone gay had raised the issue of gay rights before with him. I gave him some things to think about and I was glad about that, whatever the result.

Nothing happened soon. Although the truth set me freer, it did not get me a job right away. The governor's legal counsel did not call.

Raymond J. Flynn, who was perceived as being conservative because of his anti-school-busing past, was elected mayor of Boston. He was in fact very liberal at the beginning of his mayoralty. It seemed that he loved activists. It did not matter what you were an activist for, it was enough that you were passionate about something. Ray Flynn wanted to bring the city together and include those who had felt excluded by the previous administration. Before his inauguration he formed transition taskforces on a number of issues. I was asked to chair the transition taskforce on human rights and public safety. I was appointed because, apart from any qualifications I had as a lawyer, I was openly gay. Besides serving on the board of GLAD, I was active in a number of gay political organizations both in the city and statewide, the Boston Lesbian and Gay Political Alliance (BLGPA), the Massachusetts Lesbian and Gay Political Caucus (MLGPC), and the Massachusetts Gay Democrats.

The next year, after Ray Flynn's election in late 1984, I testified before the Boston City Council in order to create a Boston Human Rights Commission, which (unlike the then-existing Massachusetts Commission Against Discrimination) would include as part of its mandate the protection of gay people.

In March 1985 a lesbian friend of mine, Ann Maguire, the gay liaison for the mayor, called me and said, "Congratulations, Mayor Flynn has appointed you to the newly formed City of Boston Human Rights Commission. You are the gay and lesbian member."

I replied, "Thank you very much. I will get skirts for all my suits."

That same year, still with no offer from the governor, a seat on the Boston Municipal Court opened up, and this time I submitted my application. I was granted an interview with the Judicial Nominating Committee.

My interview was held at one of the bigger Boston law firms. The wait was lengthy, but finally an aide came for me. I was brought into a long conference room with a long table filled on both sides with curious faces. I felt like a monkey at a zoo.

I and some of my friends had lobbied some of the members of the Judicial Nominating Committee beforehand, but most of the people we had contacted did not seem to be there that night. Many of the members contacted asked my friends why I had to say that I am gay on the application. "Why does he have to tell us *that*?" a number of them asked my friends.

During the interview a Latina woman, who worked for a gay man (who was soon to die from AIDS), giggled and asked if I was still a model. The person next her asked her, "What kind of question is that?"

She said, still giggling, "He lists it on his application."

I replied, "No, I'm too fat."

I believe she knew that on the application I had to list every source of income from the time I started to earn money.

Then an assistant attorney general said, "If you were appointed, you would be the first . . . uh . . . uh . . . of your kind, are you prepared for the resultant publicity?"

I replied that I had already received publicity for being the gay member of the Boston Human Rights Commission, and I could handle the publicity of being appointed a judge.

Not content to leave well enough alone, he then asked, "If you were appointed, what would you do if somebody, uh . . . uh . . . of your kind appeared in front of you? Would you recuse yourself?"

"No," I said, "I wouldn't. No more than I would recuse myself when black people appeared in front of me if I were black, or if Jewish people appeared in front of me and I were Jewish." I knew he was Jewish and wanted to bring the point home. I think I overdid it.

My name did not go up to the governor as one of the three candidates for the job.

I reapplied for a judgeship in 1988, during Governor Dukakis' third term. I knew Haskell "Hacky" Kassler, a very bright, kind, and funny man who was now the chairman of a new Judicial Nominating Committee. A few years before he had been on the other side of a case from me in my job investigating lawyers. He represented a domestic relations lawyer who was being complained of. We were able to come to a mutually satisfying resolution of the case.

After I sent in the application he called me and said, "Dermot, we can interview you now or in a few months when there is an opening at the Boston Municipal Court. I would recommend that you wait until the opening because we may forget you if we do it now." Either in this conversation or in another before the interview, Hacky said to me, "I don't want you to be presented as the gay candidate. You should be viewed as a highly qualified candidate who happens to be gay."

I responded defensively, "I am not going to deny who or what I am."

He said, "No, no, no. No one is asking you to do that. Can't you tell them that it's just something . . . something you do on Saturday nights . . . like the Elks?"

I trusted Hacky Kassler, and agreed to wait until the opening was closer. In the meantime the Judicial Nominating Committee had its picture taken with representatives of most of the minority bar associations. The picture was published in *Lawyers Weekly* with an article noting how inclusive the committee was trying to be. Of course, one minority bar association was not represented, and that was the MLGBA. I called the MLGBA's chairpersons. Terry Sweeney, one of the chairs, wrote a wonderful letter to *Lawyers Weekly* and to the committee noting their lapse. The committee was genuinely embarrassed and invited Terry to meet with them, which he did. Terry softened them up for me, I suspect.

I also knew more members of this committee than I did of the prior one and I called many of them in advance. Many people outright pledged their support; those who didn't commit themselves were at least congenial.

I was interviewed in August 1988 at a different law firm, a more relaxed place than the scene of the first interview. A gay man I knew came out of the conference room as I was waiting to enter. He had just finished his interview. He recognized me and said, "They were eating supper. It only lasted about ten minutes. Good luck."

I asked, "Were you 'out' with them?"

"No, I can't be. My family lives here. My father's a cop. I wish I could. Are you?"

"Yes."

"That's brave. Good luck."

The chairman himself, Hacky Kassler, came out to get me. He said, "Don't be nervous. We're a good bunch. We have a lot of people to talk to and are trying to go right through so we may be finishing supper while we ask our questions. I hope you don't mind."

This time the questions were softballs. Somebody asked what effect the fact that I am an alcoholic in recovery would have on my work as a judge if I were appointed.

Having been to the court a few days earlier to observe it in action, I was able to talk about a case in which I would have required evaluation and treatment for the still drunk, young woman defendant who was charged with raising hell in a hospital emergency room after having gashed her leg in a barroom. She was still barefoot at the arraignment. Although the case was disposed of at arraignment, the subject of her alcohol problem never came up. One member of the Judicial Nominating Commission, later a very important appellate court judge, wondered about the constitutionality of a judge inquiring into the sobriety of people appearing in front of him, but another member who was a respected criminal defense lawyer said that was exactly what a judge should inquire about when crafting a disposition.

Another member noted that I was active in a lot of organizations; she named them, even the gay ones, and asked what I would do about them if I were appointed.

I said that I would resign from the political and advocacy organizations, as I would be required to do by the Judicial Canon of Ethics.

She smiled approvingly.

Other members commented with approval on their work with me at the Board of Bar Overseers. Another told me how much she liked my younger brother, also a lawyer.

It was a love-in.

But there is no certainty about these things. The next day I called Eleanor Mazzone, the very kind staff person to the Judicial Nominating Committee. "How did I do, Mrs. Mazzone?"

"You did very well, Dermot, but you know that you come with all kinds of baggage."

Gucci, Louis Vuitton? I wanted to ask.

"They won't decide quickly. Three names will be sent up," she added.

Governor Dukakis was running for president, and it was only August. I did not think the governor would create an issue in that campaign by appointing a gay man to a judgeship when the opposition was doing everything it could to portray him as a liberal. So I simply waited, knowing I had done my best.

Shortly after Dukakis lost the election, I received a call from Mrs. Mazzone telling me that I was one of the three finalists, and that I would be meeting with the governor. I started to campaign again. I stalked Mayor Flynn to ask him to send a letter on my behalf. He did. I called in a lot of chits and asked other people to talk to the governor, his wife, his brother-in-law.

The interview was held shortly before Christmas. Mrs. Mazzone was in the waiting room with a woman lawyer who, I had already heard, was one of my two rivals. She was quiet; perhaps that was her response to being nervous. Mine was to be jocular and chatty. A civil litigator, who I knew, walked out of the governor's office. He was the other rival. He leaned down and said to me, "I have no idea what he talked about, but it wasn't about the job. Don't expect him to talk about the job."

Then I was brought in. The governor was at the door. The legal counsel said, "This is Dermot Meagher, Governor."

The governor said, "Dermot and I have talked before." Then he paused and added, "He was one of my best students."

I liked the second sentence better than the first. I recalled our first meeting in that office five years earlier. The governor quickly put me at ease. He noted that for somebody who investigated and prosecuted lawyers, there certainly were a lot of lawyers who liked me. He commented that I had a very tough job. Then he talked about the colorful former chief justice of the Boston Municipal Court, Elijah Adlow, before whom he had appeared as a young lawyer. No commitment was made; no deadline given. He thanked me for coming. I assured him the pleasure was mine, and that was that.

On January 30, 1989, I received a call from the governor's legal counsel. " Congratulations! The Governor is nominating you for the vacancy on the Boston Municipal Court. He is sending your name to the joint bar committee. Although we do not expect any problems there, please don't tell anyone about this until you get through that committee. Then arrange to come see me about getting through the Governor's Council."

Of course, I only told my 200 closest friends.

There were two more hurdles to go, however.

Contrary to the legal counsel's belief, and to my alleged goodwill among lawyers, there was a problem with the Joint Bar Committee. That committee is composed of lawyer/representatives from the bar associations in each of the counties and of the Massachusetts Bar Association. The Joint Bar Committee was customarily sent the names of judicial candidates for review and comment. Its recommendations had no legal status but, as far as I know, only two people had been successfully nominated without its approval.

The Office of the Bar Counsel, where I worked, was at that time investigating two members of the Joint Bar Committee, and I was personally in charge of the investigation of the husband of a third member. She led the charge against me. None of these lawyers thought it necessary to disqualify himself or herself or even to notify the committee that they were being investigated. The dutiful wife was objecting because I am gay, or that was what she said. She thought it was a disgrace and had recently led a campaign to keep discrimination against gay people from being added to the Democratic party platform.

I and my supporters contacted a number of influential lawyers, including a former president of the Massachusetts Bar Association. He was horrified that these lawyers on the Joint Bar Committee were not revealing their conflicts of interest. He correctly perceived that if these shenanigans were made public, such behavior could end the Joint Bar Committee's special role in judicial nominations. The opposition quickly folded after the committee heard from him and others about their folly.

The Governor's Council was the next hurdle. The Governor's Council had its own questionnaire, which I had to fill out and which, unlike that of the Judicial Nominating Committee, was open to public examination. The questions were mainly concerned with recent political contributions and whether I was now, or ever had been, a member of the Communist Party.

I decided to campaign throughout the state, to contact people in the districts of the councilors and ask them to call the councilors and ask for their support. The gay underground helped to some degree, but more important were lawyers I had come to know in my work at the Board of Bar Overseers—not the lawyers I investigated, but the lawyers who had represented those people, as well as past and present bar overseers, who were distinguished in their communities and who could vouch for my qualifications.

The governor's councilors had never seen anyone like me before—an openly gay candidate, also admittedly alcoholic. I knew I had to work harder than other candidates. I knew that the few candidates who had been denied appointment had failed to take the councilors seriously. The councilors were elected to approve or deny judgeships and if I wanted the job, I had better pay attention to them.

Although I knew James O'Brien, the councilor from Worcester, because he was a lawyer there, and he had dated my sister, I knew he liked my father better. I did not know how I was going to ask my ailing father to call him. Instead, I asked my mother to send a note. She was eager to do that. The Worcester newspapers had announced my nomination, fulfilling one of my worst fears by announcing on the front page that I am gay. My last remaining uncle said, "I didn't know that."

I made a visit to Worcester for the purpose of asking for my father's help. My father, who was in and out of lucidity at the time, sat in his wheelchair in stony silence as the banter among the rest of the family members present played itself out. I talked about how the campaign was going.

Finally, I told my father that it would be a big help if he called Jimmy O'Brien. After some equivocation and talk from my father about how unimportant he, my father, was, I dialed Jimmy O'Brien's number. My father picked up the phone and talked to Jimmy.

"I would appreciate your support for my son," my father said.

There was a lot of talk on the other end, which we could not hear.

"What did he say?" my sister asked when our father hung up.

"The usual bullshit about what a great guy I am," he replied. "He said he'd vote for you."

And that was that.

I continued to talk to each of the councilors, as did my friends. Until I got a commitment I kept the pressure on. A priest friend solicited his parishioner who was a councilor. Congressmen and members of the Boston

City Council called. Drag queens were making calls to their councilors. It was wonderful.

A few days before the hearing, at the suggestion of a former councilor, I went to visit *my* governor's councilor, who was also the councilor for the district containing the Boston Municipal Court. I ran into his son as I entered his building.

The son, who I had known for years and who was never very political, said, "What are you doing here?"

I said, "I've been nominated for a judgeship."

The son brought me straight to see his father.

The son said, "Dad, this is Mr. Meagher. He's a friend of mine. He is being nominated for a judgeship."

His father said, "I don't care what they say about you. I'm with you 100 percent." He then listed all the people who had called him for me.

The hearing was scheduled for March 7, 1989, the feast day of Saint Thomas Aquinas—a good omen, I thought.

At the hearing before the Governor's Council, which was in the same room where in 1951 my father was sworn in as a judge of the Superior Court, the councilors asked me questions. I presented character witnesses on my behalf. Judicial candidates typically bring four or five supporters. I knew I was problematic, so I brought fifteen.

Although two of the councilors had received letters in opposition, only one person said he would testify against me. He was a lawyer I had investigated some years before, but, of course, he didn't say that, and I couldn't say it pursuant to the rules governing my office. He, too, like some of the lawyers on the Joint Bar Committee, who were also investigated by my office, thought it was a disgrace to appoint a gay man to a judgeship. He came to the hearing, but for some reason did not stay around to testify.

There was a straw vote at the end of the hearing and most of the councilors were equivocal, maybe leaning my way, except for my district's councilor, who repeated forcefully, "I'm with him 100 percent," and then again listed all the dignitaries who had called on my behalf. At the end of the list he added loudly, "And my son tells me I have to vote for him."

I almost cried. This tough, old man had enough respect for his son that he would do what the son asked. "Touched" is too weak a word.

As is the custom, the real vote was scheduled for the next week in case any new information came to light. The night before the vote, one more councilor told me he would vote for me, giving me a majority. However, the governor's office still wanted the lieutenant governor to be able to vote if she had to, so they arranged to have the governor preside.

Custom and etiquette do not permit the candidate to be present in the council's chamber for the vote. I stayed home alone. I asked two lawyer friends to watch the vote and to call me once it was complete. I knew that the council was scheduled to vote at 11:00 a.m. That time came and went. At 1:00, when I could stand it no longer, I called the office of an aide to the governor, which I knew to be near the council chamber. I asked for one of my lawyer friends. After a long wait, he came to the phone.

"Hello, Your Honor," he said. "The vote was eight to one."

After finding out who the dissenter was and after calling my mother, I got on my bicycle and rode all around the geographical jurisdiction of the Boston Municipal Court, up the riverbank to Massachusetts Avenue, through the South End into Back Bay, into downtown via Chinatown, through the North End, and home again. It was a gray and cold March day, but I did not feel it.

I still had to be sworn in. The legislature had not yet passed legislation protecting gay people from discrimination, so I did not want to have the ceremony in the House of Representatives, as was the custom. My friends at City Hall arranged to let me rent Faneuil Hall, the same place where Jack Kennedy had announced for president.

As I was preparing the event my father said to me, "You're spending a lot of money on this thing."

"Well, Dad, I'm probably not going to get married," I replied. (Gay marriage in Massachusetts was not even a twinkle in anyone's eye in 1989.) My brothers fell on the floor laughing and he harrumphed.

On May 3, 1989, Governor Dukakis swore me in. My old friend, Vin McCarthy, was the master of ceremonies. I gave a great speech (if I say so myself) acknowledging the historic importance of the occasion, and then had a very big party for the 800 guests upstairs at Faneuil Hall in the headquarters of the Ancient and Honorable Artillery.

People kept on congratulating my father, and he kept saying, "I didn't do anything." But, of course, that was not true.

Sara G. Schnorr
Admitted 1979

It didn't occur to Sara Schnorr (then Thomas Schnorr) to apply to Harvard when she was graduating from the all-boys Catholic high school she attended in Pittsburgh. She imagined that she would attend college somewhere in western Pennsylvania, where she had grown up with an alcoholic father who wasn't around a lot. Schnorr was smart and accomplished and she was sure of one thing: she wanted to grow up to be everything her father was not. This, she has clearly accomplished. After her mother's death several years ago, she discovered a journal where her mother noted that her father had gone through fifteen jobs in one year; Schnorr has worked at Edwards Wildman for over thirty-five years.

Encouraged by a fellow Eagle Scout who was a freshman at Harvard, Schnorr did apply and, to her surprise, was accepted. Attending Harvard made a huge difference in her life, and she will acknowledge it opened many doors for her. Upon graduation, she was awarded a Fulbright and studied linguistics and philosophy for a year in Germany before returning to graduate school at Wesleyan. Schnorr taught high school for four years before making the decision to go to law school. She was in her late twenties at the time and recently married.

In 1979, she graduated from the University of Virginia School of Law. Offered jobs at both Palmer & Dodge and Edwards & Angell, she chose to return to Palmer & Dodge, where she'd been a summer clerk, and has remained there ever since, focusing her practice on real estate acquisition, development, land use, affordable housing, and financing matters. It was with no small irony that she watched as the two firms later merged to form Edwards Wildman.

Schnorr married and she and her wife ultimately adopted two children. Early on in the marriage, Schnorr (then Thomas), shared with her wife that she was struggling with her gender identity. For years, Schnorr went through a series of unsuccessful therapeutic attempts to "cure" her. As she approached her sixtieth birthday, Schnorr finally came to the realization that she needed to transition. For her family, this was extremely difficult and, although Schnorr and her wife remain close, the first year after she transitioned was fraught with sadness and turmoil for the family.

One of her children took the news with ease and, in fact, thought it was "cool." The other child had a hard time looking at Schnorr after she'd had surgery, and it was a major victory when he agreed to go out in public with his father, who was now a woman. Schnorr tells a wonderful story about this outing. Schnorr had tickets to a Bruins game. When they got to the game, her son was very nervous, thinking perhaps "that everyone would know that I used to be a man." A man sitting behind them tapped her son on the shoulder and said, "It's really great that your mom takes you to a game!" Her son now says he sometimes wishes she hadn't transitioned, but that he still loves her.

In sharp contrast, Schnorr's experience in dealing with her transition at work has been amazingly supportive. Schnorr loves her law practice and certainly did not want to risk losing her career. Many people who transition as older adults leave their homes, families, and jobs to start over somewhere new; she did not want this for herself. She considered moving to a smaller firm and she thought her interviews with two firms went well. She was open about her transition to both firms and basically got the same answer: they really liked her; they needed to do the math to figure out whether it made economic sense. She later learned that two of the senior partners in one firm were very active in the Catholic Archdiocese of Boston and felt that having a transgender partner would present an unacceptable risk for them.

For years before her transition, Edwards Wildman Palmer & Dodge (EAPD) had an antidiscrimination policy that included sexual orientation and gender identity. After consulting with an employment attorney, who reviewed Schnorr's partnership agreement and firm policies, Schnorr was told, "The good news is your firm has great policies; the uncertain news is that while those policies protect employees, they might not protect partners." In 2009, when Schnorr was preparing to transition, there were no protections for transgender people in the law. Aware that her partners could remove her as a partner, but determined to move forward, her attorney helped her craft an e-mail to the managing partner and management committee essentially alerting them that she was taking steps to transition to living as a woman and she hoped that she would have the support of the firm. Late in the evening on a Thursday, "I hit 'send' and crossed my fingers."

The next morning she checked her e-mail and, by 9:00 a.m., had received supportive responses from nearly half the management committee. When she set up meetings with her three most significant clients to tell them she was transitioning, she was worried that they would seek new counsel. The opposite happened: the clients were more concerned about losing Schnorr's representation. Hugely relieved by both her firm's response and her clients' responses, Schnorr mapped out a plan with the human resources department about how to handle the transition. Schnorr was acutely aware that other transgender people are not so fortunate as to have such a supportive work environment.

Schnorr wrote an e-mail to her partners, and later to the entire staff as well as to a couple of hundred contacts in the Boston real estate and community development community. In the e-mail to the staff, she wrote:

> Over the last 6 or 7 months, many of you have noticed some quite obvious physical changes in me, and some of you occasionally inquired what was going on. My proffered response was light-hearted but far from the truth, and I now want to be honest and open with all of you . . . . When I return to the office in December, I would ask you to do your best to call me Sara and use female

pronouns when talking to or about me. I understand that many of you may find this difficult and awkward and it may take some time to adjust . . . . Since I graduated from law school more years ago than I care to admit, P&D, and now EAPD, has been my only home as a lawyer. I've forged lasting and truly wonderful personal friendships and professional relationships with many past and present firm lawyers and staff. I want to personally thank Walter [Reed], my partners, and the firm's senior administrative staff for the acceptance, support and help they've given me in implementing my transition to Sara. That speaks volumes about the fundamental humanity and decency of EAPD as an organization.

EAPD management sent an e-mail to the entire firm to express their full support: "The Firm is committed to providing a professional, collegial and respectful environment for all personnel within our diverse Firm, and will do so for Sara." During her medical leave, the human resources department offered trainings to educate staff. As soon as Schnorr had legally changed her name and gender, the firm took care of making the necessary administrative changes.

When she returned to the firm following her recovery from the first surgery, people were wonderful and kind, although occasionally she still is called the wrong pronoun or the wrong name. It's hard to break those habits, but Schnorr says that the reception has been more positive than she ever would have prayed for.

One unexpected revelation for Schnorr has to do with another type of discrimination. Living as a woman, Schnorr now has direct experience of how women are sometimes treated in the workplace. At a recent law school reunion, she commiserated with two female classmates about this. "They tell women we're being over-sensitive. We're not."

During the lobbying for the Massachusetts transgender rights bill, Schnorr wanted to be of help. Initially, she was discouraged from offering public testimony. It was important to demonstrate to legislators that transgender people were being demonized as a group and her story didn't show that. Ultimately, though, Schnorr testified; it had become clear that legislators needed to hear from different people with different histories, in order to appreciate the breadth of experience of the transgender community.

A colleague recently shared Schnorr's transition story with a couple devastated over the news that their daughter intended to transition to live full-time as a man. The couple was visibly relieved to know that people can succeed even if they change gender; the person is still the same person. Schnorr would say, though, that she is not exactly the same person. She's more outgoing, more assertive, and happier.

Schnorr has been involved with the Committee on Sexual Orientation and Gender Identity of the American Bar Association. She reports that, of the approximately 400,000 members, only two-tenths of 1 percent are openly LGBT. "When you think about the percentage in the general population [approximately 3.8 percent of Americans are openly LGBT], that's an awful lot of closeted people in the legal profession."

Hon. Maureen H. Monks
Admitted 1985

When Maureen Monks was a student at Boston University Law School in the early 1980s, she was told that "they had a gay student group here . . . but she left." Monks herself was openly lesbian in law school and helped to (re)form the LGBT student group. They had to request funding from student government, and despite the conservative atmosphere, they received it. She recalls that the perception was that it was more difficult for gay men to be out than for lesbians. The law school atmosphere was a competitive one in which anything other than a Wall Street career was considered "alternative," and it was generally believed that gay men had more to lose. It was not an easy atmosphere in which to be openly gay, and being out on your resumé was just not an option. Turns out that Monks' class gave the Commonwealth two of its openly gay judges: Monks herself and Mark D. Mason, appointed to the District Court in 2009.

Upon graduation in 1985, Monks worked for three years at a plaintiff's personal injury firm. She did not go out of her way to come out to her employer, but when she ran into him outside the office—accompanied by her then girlfriend—he guessed. Fortunately, it was not an issue for him. During this time (the mid-1980s) Monks became involved with a small but growing support group called Lesbians in the Law (LIL). Lawyers, paralegals, any lesbian women working in the legal profession, were welcome to join the group. LIL was primarily a social group that held monthly potluck dinners at private homes. Although there were discussions of the law and the women's experiences at work, it was not a group that had ambition to do anything more overtly political. Most of the women were closeted at work and when Monks raised the issue of sharing their very protected mailing list with the newly formed Massachusetts Lesbian and Gay Bar Association(MLGBA), she was met with resistance. One woman mused that "we already have an advocacy group—the Women's Bar Association. Why would we need another one?"

One of the members of LIL, Sandy Smales, approached Monks about joining the Women's Law Collective, a small firm in Cambridge's Central Square. It was at the Women's Law Collective that Monks met Attorney Chris Butler, with whom she ultimately formed a long professional association, ultimately changing the firm to Butler & Monks, the Women's Law Collective. They worked together for almost twenty years until Monks was appointed to the bench. Butler & Monks was known for many things, not the least of which was the firm's commitment to representing LGBT individuals and families. Butler & Monks was also one of the only firms in Massachusetts to consistently offer a sliding scale fee structure, enabling low-income individuals, LGBT people among them, to receive legal representation.

In 1987, Monks applied for a teaching job in the Battered Women's Advocacy Project at Suffolk University Law School and made a conscious decision not to come out on her resumé. With no state statutory prohibition against discrimination yet in effect and not wanting to jeopardize how the program would be treated by the University, she felt uncomfortable being out. Once hired, she came out.

In the early days of MLGBA, Monks became a board member. Later, as secretary and then cochair of the board, Monks recalls that the bar association at the time was keenly focused on getting the gay rights bill passed. The AIDS crisis was pressing in on the community, quite literally in many instances, where important gay rights organizations were losing their leadership and membership to AIDS. During her time on the board, MLGBA became an official affiliated bar association with the Massachusetts Bar Association.

Gaining professional recognition from the mainstream legal community was a huge step forward and certainly a far cry from the very beginning, when MLGBA put notices in *Lawyers Weekly* in an attempt to build what was then a tiny membership. Especially before 1989, when the antidiscrimination law was passed, many LGBT individuals were very reluctant to join a group as public as MLGBA. The organization put energy into influencing employers to be proactive in hiring LGBT attorneys and in promoting diverse and inclusive work environments. The MLGBA was proactive in encouraging communities to pass domestic partnership ordinances and in promoting the appointment of openly gay people to the bench. A little more than twenty years later, MLGBA (now known as the Massachusetts LGBTQ Bar Association) has a strong and growing membership.

In 1989, when Dermot Meagher was appointed as the first openly gay judge in the Commonwealth, "it was a big deal," Monks remembers. The appointment of Linda Giles, the first openly lesbian judge in the Commonwealth, just two years later, was equally impressive. It took a great deal of courageous leadership to move things forward for the LGBT legal community, Monks mused. Every victory, large or small, helped. Monks recalled an experience she had with another attorney in the early 1990s. Her client was a fragile mother of two small children who was in a custody battle with her husband. His claim for custody was that the mother was gay and promiscuous. While it was accurate that she was gay—this was, after all, why she wanted a divorce from her husband—she was certainly not promiscuous. The husband was represented by a prominent attorney, who was an aggressive advocate for his client. When Monks called the attorney to discuss the case, he said, "Maureen, I'm just meeting with a couple of clients here." Monks suggested she call back at a more convenient time. To her shock, he launched into details about the case in front of his clients. When Monks informed him that she thought it inappropriate for him to be talking about the case in front of other clients, he insinuated that she was having an affair with her client. She hung up. Despite there having been some clear court decisions even at the time about the impact of a parent's sexual orientation on custody matters, there was a great deal of ignorance in the legal community.[2] This same lawyer, early on in the case, told Monks, "I think your client's a lesbian—she can't possibly be asking for custody."

Family service officers (FSOs, now called probation officers) at the court suffered from the same lack of information and, sadly, this was sometimes reflected in the way LGBT litigants were treated in the courts. FSOs would meet with litigants and attorneys in an effort to help them resolve their dispute, but LGBT litigants were, at best, often misunderstood. Although Monks believes that this was due to a lack of education rather than malicious intent, it still proved difficult. "People do not realize how their subconscious prejudice impacts their actions." Fortunately, Monks remarked, things have changed rather dramatically. The law has come to recognize LGBT rights and the courts have become familiar with LGBT individuals and families. She rarely sees or experiences any signs of bias within the court system.

In one of the first (of many) contested custody trials Monks was involved with, she represented another young mother who was coming out. In his report, the guardian ad litem stated that despite all indications that the children had a healthy and close bond with their mother, the father should get custody because he could provide a more traditional household. Monks hired an expert who challenged that recommendation and, in the end, the judge—an older, conservative Catholic—recognized the strong bond of the children with their mother and ordered that the children be in her custody.

"It takes more than education, it takes a lot of personal courage" for people to put themselves on the line in the courts, says Monks. She points to the plaintiff couples in the *Goodridge* case, remarking that marriage for same-sex couples would not be the law in Massachusetts if these brave individuals had not stepped up.[3]

Monks believes that it is because of her involvement in LGBT and domestic violence advocacy that she was nominated to the bench in 2008. Monks' application moved along smoothly enough until her hearing before the Governor's Council. She was openly lesbian and had the support of the MLGBA; she enjoyed a terrific reputation within the legal community. At the hearing, one of the councilors questioned her involvement in teaching a class at Newton North High School, implying that Monks was somehow indoctrinating unsuspecting teenagers about LGBT issues. As it turned out, it was an adult education class, the purpose of which was to educate LGBT adults about their legal rights; the class met, in the evening, at Newton North High School. Monks' nomination was approved by the council (without that particular councilor's vote).

Things have changed even in the years since her appointment. In 2014 there are just under thirty openly lesbian or gay judges on the bench in the Commonwealth. In 2008 the number of openly LGBT judges was in the teens. And before 1989, that number was zero.

Hon. Paula M. Carey
Admitted 1986

Although Paula Carey knew other professionals who were anxious about being outed, she did not share that anxiety. At the same time, she did not see the need to make grand pronouncements about her sexual orientation. As she will tell you, "I just lived my life."

Carey worked as a business analyst at Dun & Bradstreet for four years before leaving for law school. Dun & Bradstreet had offered to fund her law school education, but Carey knew she did not want to return to work in that field and did not feel right accepting their offer. Instead, she funded her own law school education, working throughout law school to pay her way. That did not leave much time for other things, and even if she'd known an LGBT student group had existed, she probably wouldn't have had the time to be involved.

After graduation from New England School of Law in 1986, Carey practiced first at Arthur & Jaworski, and then at her own firm, Carey & Mooney. She practiced family law for over twenty years before being appointed to the Probate and Family Court by then-Governor Paul Cellucci in 2001. Carey was out during the process of her application to the bench and introduced her partner before the Governor's Council.

Her partner stood with her on the podium at her swearing in.

The *Lawyers Weekly* editorial applauding her appointment made reference to Carey's partner, openly acknowledging that she was in a same-sex relationship. Carey assumes that some people may have been concerned about her ability to be impartial, but Carey's reputation as an honest and straightforward judge easily dispelled this notion. Her hard work and dedication resulted in her eventual elevation to the post of chief justice of the Massachusetts Trial Court in 2013.

While she was chief of the Probate and Family Court, Carey recalls hearing about an incident that occurred at one county court's holiday party where the subject of openly gay judges came up. Apparently, a judge was overheard to say that "all you have to be is gay or lesbian to be a judge." As chief, it was Carey's job to do something about this. Knowing that there were LGBT individuals who work in that court and determined that they should feel safe in the workplace, she felt it imperative to discipline the judge in question.

Carey would agree that the evolution in the law protecting the rights of the LGBT community has made the legal profession easier to be in. So much so that in her current capacity as chief justice of the Trial Court, she feels free to focus on other serious issues facing the courts, such as addiction and its impact on families and the criminal justice system. Carey's commitment to her work is evident and she'll admit she feels very lucky. She acknowledges that sometimes you need a thick skin to get through whatever bias may be floating around, but what is important is for lawyers to focus on being good lawyers, ethical and honorable. The rest will follow.

Mary L. Bonauto
Admitted 1987

(This interview has been adapted from an interview conducted by Elizabeth A. Brown, Esq., for Breaking Barriers: The Unfinished Story of Women Lawyers and Judges *(MCLE, Inc. 2012)).*

How did you decide to become a lawyer?

I decided to become a lawyer when I was a teenager. It had a lot to do with being underdog identified, if you will. . . . Even as a young person, it was not hard to discern vast inequalities and I wanted to do something to try to level the playing fields for people from all walks of life. My perspectives became more informed and nuanced with time, but there is no doubt that "the law" is a powerful structural force shaping what we value, and what is possible, and for whom.

Where do you think you got that sense of right and wrong and compelling justice?

Someday I will figure all that out. First of all, the real people I meet, talk to, and represent are the heart and soul of why we work to make "liberty and justice for all" a lived reality, and as soon as possible. Looking back, my parents taught my brothers and me about respect for others and the dignity and value of all persons—with no exceptions. I was also raised as a Catholic, and the social justice emphasis in Catholicism influenced me enormously. I attended public schools in a somewhat distressed area through high school, and I grew up knowing about people's struggles. And of course, like many people, I've experienced the sting of imposed otherness, both subtly and blatantly—whether because my last name ends in a vowel, or because my background and circumstances were different from others, or because I wasn't behaving properly "for a woman," or because of my sexual orientation. The upside of these experiences is that I learned how current societal norms can contort the basic values we share, such as living the Golden Rule and liberty and equality for all. My years of work at GLAD have only widened and deepened my perspectives on "justice for all." I should be clear, though, that I feel like my cup runneth over in terms of blessings. I am not complaining. The challenge is how to give back when I have been given so much.

How did you decide to go into law, as opposed to say, being a union organizer or taking another professional path?

There are many issues about which I am passionate beyond the work I do at GLAD, and law can be a tool in addressing many of them. I didn't know lawyers growing up . . . but I saw law as involving both big systems and big ideas and I was (and am) very interested in the role of law in establishing rules and norms by which we live. . . . I read about lawyers and historical conflicts. For example, in middle school, I became very taken with Abraham Lincoln, including how he evolved over time to recognize that slavery intolerably clashed with our basic constitutional values. Reading a biography of Justice Oliver Wendell Holmes, Jr., impressed upon me the necessity of our constitutional commitment to free speech in a diverse and sometimes disagreeable society. I came to understand the genius of the framers in setting forth enduring principles that would take shape in a dynamic and evolving society, rather than creating a rule book of eighteenth-century standards.

Did you have any role models when you were in law school or starting out who were female?

I have been lucky. I have learned from so many people over the years, starting with my immediate and extended families. Part of it was simply that they believed in me. Both of my parents are, and all of my grandparents were, hardworking people with outsized integrity and down-to-earth practicality. Others inspired me to do what I loved regardless of perceived practicality. One of my comparative literature professors at Hamilton College, Nancy Rabinowitz, nurtured my love of classical Greek and helped me to think critically about everything.

How does it feel to be compared to Thurgood Marshall?

I appreciate the compliment, but the comparison just doesn't work. What is great is the principles of liberty and equality that generations and generations of Americans have relied on in our state and federal constitutions. We've now had decades of work—not only of lawyers but in every branch of government and with the all-important public—to ensure that there are no sexual orientation and gender-identity based exceptions to the pledge of "equal justice under law."

Do you have a goal for your career, and how do you think about what you want to accomplish in your career?

I'm not ambitious—traditionally ambitious . . . about a career, per se. . . . After I went to law school, I wanted to jump into working directly with people right away, so I did not want to clerk (something I would now do differently). I took a job with a midsized law firm in Maine; I was their eighth lawyer. The firm's anchor partners had previously done civil rights work. They wanted me to make money, but they also let me loose to pursue my own interests. I signed up through the Volunteer Lawyers Project for pro bono work, but because it was the late 1980s, I found myself immersed in the AIDS crisis as well. Now that I look back on it, I can see that the work I did then was a model for what we do at GLAD. At that time, there was massive fear and discrimination . . . to the point that if you were suspected of being gay, some people would assume you had AIDS, and invariably, negative consequences would follow. I threw myself into helping individuals contest job discrimination when they were summarily fired for their presumed HIV status and also with end-of-life planning in a hurry. And I worked on systemic issues, helping state legislators craft insurance laws in light of the epidemic. It turned out that I was one of the few out lawyers in the entire State of Maine at that time. That meant business! I'm not saying that only a gay or lesbian lawyer could meet people's legal needs, but many people simply felt more comfortable with me at that point. I negotiated "moral turpitude" clauses out of employment contracts, helped young people emancipate themselves legally when their parents kicked them out of the house, and pressed the police to be more responsive to anti-gay violence.

But then . . . in November 1989, Governor Dukakis signed the . . . second law in the entire country, forbidding discrimination based on sexual orientation in employment, housing, public accommodations, and credit. And GLAD, where I work now, started advertising for a lawyer to enforce that law. I saw the ad . . . and I talked to my partner and said, "That's what I really want to do." She said to go for it. I applied, thinking GLAD would never hire me. I was . . . two years out of law school, and I assumed they would hire somebody with far more experience for such an important job. But in 1990, they hired me. At the time, I thought I would go do the job for two years, by the end of which I would be utterly exhausted and would then return to private practice. But after two years, I was just getting started. I'd barely scratched the surface of what I saw needed to be done. So I stayed.

I have thought about my career in terms of the goal of eliminating that gap that exists between the law and the law as applied to gay people (and others) as opposed to achieving any particular position. I think a person's sexual orientation and gender identity is and should be irrelevant to his or her rights, freedoms and opportunities; it's just another articulation of the pledge of "equal justice under law." Without a doubt, that gap has narrowed in my time at GLAD, and I'd like to stay at GLAD until . . . that gap no longer exists and people can live their lives without internal or external barriers posted by who they are.

What are you proudest of in your life? I'll broaden it, rather than just your career. What are some of the things that you are proudest of having accomplished at this point in your existence?

I don't know if I would say proud, but I am just so grateful that I've been able to have my family that I have.

How old are your girls?

They were born in 2001. . . . I've been with my partner, Jennifer Wriggins, since 1987and we've been through a lot together. . . .

Can you talk a little bit about balancing work and family?

As everyone knows, it is so difficult.

It is so difficult. Do you have any thoughts, do you have any advice, do you have any observations, having done it now for quite some time? Does it get any easier with time?

For all the joy in being a parent, it's still hard work. I have just come to accept that I am going to be extra tired for a number of years. Jenny and I both committed to being the best parents we can be and having a strong relationship with them. But inevitably, there are also just times when you are more pressured, you're on a deadline, and it is harder to be as present and as focused, and that can last for too long. It bothers me, but I also try to remember that overall, they have great lives, with lots of love and joy, and they know in their bones that they are deeply loved and respected by us. It helps enormously that GLAD has come to be an incredibly flexible employer, allowing me to work odd hours at times so I can chaperone an occasional school field trip or deal with the blizzard of appointments and activities. GLAD also understands that I will not be able to do everything I did before Jenny and I had children. That is hard for me to accept, but like all parents, you see that the constancy of children is change, and that means some things are possible now that were not when they were much younger.

Can you talk about a case or two of which you are particularly proud?

On the one hand, the marriage cases are huge because being able to marry the person you love transforms your life. In point of fact, the *Goodridge v. Department of Public Health* [440 Mass. 309. (2003)] case from Massachusetts broke an historic barrier. Chief Justice Marshall and her colleagues are rightly hailed for the courage to live up to our constitutional commitments. Yet, paving the way also meant that many people had a share of grief that people in other states have not—the plaintiffs, the courts, the legislature, the governor, and the citizenry as a whole. I am so proud of and eternally grateful to all of those in Massachusetts who made that victory possible, and the many who made it secure when the legislature rejected the last of the proposed constitutional amendments to reverse *Goodridge* in June 2007. At the same time, I've worked on myriad cases that are consequential for the parties and also establish principles about how sexual orientation should not matter in terms of freedoms, rights and opportunities. I am thinking of cases involving blatant antigay discrimination in jobs, and in places of public accommodation, and how the legal process helped restore people's dignity and also reminded businesses to discard outdated attitudes about gay people.

I'm thinking of cases where parents felt intense vulnerability about having no legal connection to their child, and how GLAD's cases were vehicles for moving the law closer to familial realities, by establishing joint adoptions, or joint guardianship or de facto parenthood. There are plenty of times when I've handled a case that that doesn't change life for everyone, but the effect is still profound. . . .

How, if at all, do you think being female has affected the way you practice law? And I don't know . . . if it would be better to ask you . . . is there a way to separate being gay from being female?

There's me as a woman, and there's me as a lesbian.

First of all, I was always taught to be a "nice girl." I had to learn that being nice didn't mean I had to listen to another attorney berate or ridicule me or my legal position. All the same, it is no disservice to your client to press that client's interests in a pleasant manner and to extend basic courtesies to other counsel.

Second, I realize that for some people, dealing with me also means conjuring up their attitudes about gay people. For some, and increasingly, that's no big deal. But to this day, for others it means an automatic discounting of my legal analysis and credibility. Others believe they can simply intone the name of where I work—"Gay & Lesbian Advocates & Defenders"—and that affiliation is indictment enough. Being lesbian, gay, bisexual, or transgender is still stigmatized, and it was that much more so when I started out. I recall making an oral argument early on during which a justice seemed hidden behind a Redweld file on the bench and peered out over his papers to look at me. I'm not a mind reader, but I believe this judge was spending more time thinking about who and what I was than about my legal argument. I still have experiences like that, but overall, there's been a sea change in attitudes.

Another thing which you know from having now met me is that I'm five feet, two inches tall. And I don't have a very loud voice. It's easy for people to underestimate you in those circumstances, especially when you're female. . . . I think there was a period of time where I was underestimated by my opponents. . . . There's a way in which winning *Goodridge* blew my cover, so to speak. . . . And then I wasn't underestimated quite so much.

How did that change? How did people approach you differently? How did you sense that people interacted with you differently?

We've always had productive collaborations with private practice attorneys, and winning *Goodridge* brought more offers to partner with us. There is more respect that we know what we're talking about—about the law, about timing, about strategy. On a personal level, people project onto you. I recognize that it is an awesome gift and responsibility to be able to talk about the constitution's meaning for the lives of gay and transgender people and for same-sex relationships. But I am still the same person trying to get her work to a place where she can get home in time to have dinner with her kids. . . .

So it sounds like there were times in your career where you felt like you sensed some disrespect. How do you deal with that? Because I think that's something that a lot of women in law face.

I don't dwell on that. GLAD maintains high standards about lawyering and how we interact with others. You have to vent sometimes, and then let it roll off of your back. So essentially . . . that old saying—[a] woman has to work twice as hard to be thought of as half as good—that's been true for me as a woman, but it's also been true for us at GLAD. We care about getting things right, and it shows. What would be hard is to face disrespect among one's colleagues and that is not a problem we have at GLAD.

What would you attribute the sea change that's occurred in the last twenty-some years to?

A number of factors, and one of them . . . is the nondiscrimination law that was enacted at the end of 1989. It was a seventeen-year struggle to pass a law stating, in effect, that a person should be judged based on the job they do and not their sexual orientation and that an employer can't toss them out of a job upon discovering that they're gay. This marked a turning point in the sense that gay people went from being outsiders who could be treated poorly at will, to actually having some measure of legal protection based on who they are. And then of course, there were other important changes in the law, particularly the 2003 Supreme Court decision, *Lawrence v. Texas*, where the Court struck down all remaining sodomy laws on the basis that gay people enjoy equal liberty under the U.S. Constitution as well.

Setting aside the legal reasoning, *Lawrence* was important in Massachusetts, even though we were not enforcing our sodomy law.[4] . . . When those laws exist, there's an imputation of criminality. And when I started at GLAD, I remember many times being asked if it was illegal to be gay . . . which of course it was not criminal to be gay. . . . But the imputation of criminality clearly put gay people beyond the pale and the reach of the law. The 1989 Massachusetts nondiscrimination law began to change that, and there were other changes after '89 as well. But then when you get to 2003, and the Supreme Court's saying, we were wrong in 1986, and we are overruling *Bowers v. Hardwick*[5] as wrong when it was decided, and wrong today because the Constitution does not permit laws that demean the dignity of gay people, then that brings gay people into the law in a whole new way. . . .

The sea change has also been in our larger culture's slow awakening from seeing gay people . . . as outsiders to be regarded with hostility and suspicion to seeing us as ordinary people who are simply seeking to participate in and contribute to the same society that we share in common. And it seems so simple, and . . . so boring, but that's really what has been happening since I started doing this work full-time, [over] twenty years ago. . . . We have a ways to go, and we are far from the time when our culture, legal systems, and fellow travelers regard one's sexual orientation and gender identity are a nonissue.

What do you love about your practice?

I work with a very talented and committed group of people, who have stratospherically high legal and ethical standards, who care deeply about people, and who are as respectful and supportive as they can be about their colleagues' family lives. . . . GLAD has been listed as one of the best law firms to work at in Massachusetts. I think it's because we do interesting and important work, and we're always facing new challenges and learning on the job. We're completely aligned with our clients in terms of our shared goals. . . . We will do what it takes to move forward, even though, as people often tell us, it looks impossible. . . . We even have fun. I'm at an intersection of law, politics, and policy where I can use the legal tools I have to . . . establish new precedents of fairness. It's extremely exciting. It's another example of how my cup runneth over. . . . I feel very fortunate.

Robert L. Quinan
Admitted 1989

As a summer associate at Bingham, Dana & Gould in 1987, Rob Quinan was asked to work on behalf of the firm's client, Life Insurance Association of Massachusetts. The Association was suing the state insurance agency charged with regulating insurance coverage for HIV/AIDS-related care. One of the regulations the client wanted to challenge concerned the ability of the insurer to gather information from applicants for life insurance about their HIV status. Conflicted by his instinct to be protective of the rights of HIV-positive individuals, while at the same time understanding of the need to properly advocate for the client, Quinan chose to see this as an opportunity to persuade the client of a more moderate approach. In the end, Quinan's work resulted in the protection of confidentiality for HIV-positive individuals and at the same time satisfied the client's need for information.

While in law school at Georgetown (Class of 1988), Quinan had been involved in the LGBT student group. As it happened, his arrival in law school coincided with the group's lawsuit against the University seeking official recognition and the funding that came with that recognition. The

LGBT student group prevailed. Quinan was out as a gay man in law school but when he spent the summer of 1987 at Bingham, and even later when he was hired as an associate, he did not feel comfortable announcing this to his coworkers. Working on the insurance regulation case during that summer, Quinan walked the fine line of advocating for the right to confidentiality of LGBT individuals while being careful to maintain his own right to confidentiality. It seems that Quinan had a knack for being in the right place at the right time, for in his first year at Bingham, the gay rights bill came before the Massachusetts legislature. After seventeen years of being considered by the legislature, it appeared that the bill actually had a chance of passing in 1989. Quinan, who was very involved with working for passage of the bill, explained that "the right-wingers were threatening to put forward a ballot question if the bill passed." In the midst of figuring out how to come out while not jeopardizing his career, Quinan was asked by the then-fledgling MLGBA to write the brief to the Supreme Judicial Court to defeat the ballot initiative. Quinan approached the only openly gay partner at the firm, Randall (Randy) Farrar, to seek his advice as to whether to write the brief. Randy encouraged him to do so, believing that this was a legitimate pro bono activity for the firm. Gary Buseck of GLAD spearheaded the effort to defeat the ballot question, Quinan wrote the amicus brief on behalf of the bar association, and the ballot initiative was defeated.

In 1990, Quinan was asked to join the MLGBA board and later participated in a program sponsored by the Massachusetts Bar Association (MBA) with attorney Nancy Shilepsky and others regarding the future of the Massachusetts Commission Against Discrimination. He was becoming more and more visible as an openly gay man in the legal community. The Bingham holiday party was approaching and, although Quinan invited his boyfriend at the time, his boyfriend was too nervous about being outed and declined the invitation. Instead, Quinan invited his sister, whose name tag identified her as Betsy Quinan. Quinan introduced Betsy as his sister throughout the evening but it later became apparent that not everyone understood their relationship. A small but growing group of lesbian and gay attorneys at the firm were organizing a potluck dinner hosted by one of the partners. When this partner informed two lesbians that he was inviting Quinan, they were shocked and—pointing to Betsy's presence at the holiday party—insisted that he was not gay and was, in fact, married to Betsy. The women were visibly shaken and suggested that Quinan was a spy from management trying to root out LGBT lawyers at the firm. Ultimately, Quinan was able to reassure them that he *was* actually gay, but Quinan saw that the level of paranoia then present at the firm was palpable. Quinan understood this all too well. As a student in junior high school, he was bullied for being gay. After that experience, he retreated to a closeted existence throughout high school.

By the end of his first year at Bingham, Quinan was out to his colleagues. He remained at the firm for several years, eventually managing the firm's pro bono department.

At some point, he realized that big firm lawyering was not for him. Although he had no direct experience of homophobia at the firm, Quinan had the nagging feeling that, had he remained, the opportunity for a partnership would be limited for him because of unconscious bias.

At an MLGBA annual dinner in 1993, Quinan met Attorney Alec Gray, then general counsel at the Department of Social Services (DSS, now the Department of Children and Families). As it turned out, this was a fortuitous meeting, not only because of the friendship between the two men that developed but also because there was a vacancy at DSS. Quinan submitted his resumé, for the first time with his LGBT activities revealed, and was hired. Throughout his time at DSS, Quinan worked closely with Alec, and experienced no homophobia within the agency. Quinan's work at DSS involved a great deal of appellate work through which he began to have a great deal of contact with the Massachusetts Attorney General's Office.

In another fortuitous meeting, Quinan met then–Attorney General Scott Harshbarger at a gay pride brunch and, feeling emboldened, told Harshbarger that he'd like to work for him. Harshbarger was receptive and invited him to send a resumé. Soon after, Quinan was hired to work in the Family and Community Crimes Bureau, where he remained for about two years. When Harshbarger ran for governor, Quinan moved over to the Government Bureau, where he has now worked for over fifteen years. Quinan is currently one of five managers in the Government Bureau. It was a relatively short period of time between 1987 when he was a closeted summer associate at Bingham and his application six years later in 1993 to DSS, but in that time, Quinan found support from individuals within the LGBT legal community, not to mention the passage of the then relatively new antidiscrimination law, to be out in the legal community.

Although Quinan experienced no specific homophobia within government agencies or in the courts, he has faced challenges. In the late 1990s, when he served on the Massachusetts Bar Association Board of Delegates, there was a discussion on repeal of the state sodomy law. Extremely anxious about speaking against the sodomy law in such a forum, Quinan nevertheless forged ahead. To his relief, his speech was well received and not a single person spoke against the repeal.

When the *Goodridge* case came before the court in 2002, he was at the Attorney General's Office. The plaintiffs, represented by GLAD, were suing the Department of Public Health. Judy Yogman, his supervisor at the time, sought volunteers to take the case and no one came forward. Attorney Yogman assigned the case to herself, explaining that "I would never force anyone to work on this."

At the time, Quinan's partner Steve—with whom he had entered into a Vermont civil union—was not a U.S. citizen. They felt quite vulnerable and worried that Steve would not be able to remain in the country. The ability to marry—and the ultimate downfall of the federal Defense of Marriage Act—had special meaning for Quinan and his partner.

Yogman, acknowledging that novel issues were presented in *Goodridge*, did thorough research. With the help of others in the Attorney General's Office, Quinan among them, Yogman deflected efforts by right-wing groups to intervene or influence the arguments. To some extent, however, she was influenced enough to make an argument in favor of heterosexuals being better parents. When the inevitable blowback came on this issue—after all, Massachusetts had already affirmed the rights of the LGBT community to parent in decisions such as *Adoption of*

Tammy and *ENO v. LMM*—Yogman was persuaded to abandon that argument and focus instead on the argument that this was a matter for legislature, not the courts.[6] The Attorney General's Office continued to resist homophobic elements from becoming parties to the case.

After the *Goodridge* decision affirming the right to marry, litigation ensued addressing whether city clerks would be forced to perform same-sex couples' marriages. Then-Governor Mitt Romney famously attempted to eviscerate the decision and then–Attorney General Thomas Reilly refused to participate in these efforts or in the efforts of others opposed to the decision to use the federal courts in an attempt to overturn the decision.

Quinan confirms that throughout this period, from the passage of the gay rights bill through the *Goodridge* decision, in law firms, on Beacon Hill, and in government agencies, LGBT lawyers and their allies worked hard to raise the consciousness of those integrally involved in preserving and protecting LGBT civil rights. With the passage of the gay rights bill and the subsequent positive court decisions came a level of growing comfort for LGBT lawyers in the bar and on the bench.

Hon. Angela M. Ordoñez
Admitted 1990

Angela Ordoñez graduated from Northeastern University School of Law in 1989. The first time she took the bar exam, she failed. Already working at Greater Boston Legal Services (GBLS), she discovered that four other women of color at GBLS who were recent graduates had also failed the bar exam. Although it was traumatic at the time, she redoubled her efforts and she and the other women studied hard. Determined never to have to take the bar exam again, Ordoñez put up a sign to encourage them: "NEVER AGAIN." "Never again" became a reality when all five women passed and GBLS celebrated their success with a champagne reception. Ordoñez continued at GBLS in the family law unit for almost three years.

From her vantage point as the recently appointed chief justice of the Probate and Family Court, Ordoñez can smile about this now. She has shared this experience publicly over the years—and more than one attorney has thanked her for doing so.

Judge Ordoñez herself was born to a single mother and had compassion for her clients at GBLS. Ordoñez met her wife, Carol, around this same time. Although she didn't normally share her personal life with clients, Ordoñez was comfortable being out to her coworkers. In 1993, encouraged by colleagues who worked for the Probate and Family Court, she applied for and was surprised to be offered a job as assistant register, a job she was very intrigued by. She recalls how hard it was leave the level of comfort she had in the diverse environment at GBLS; she was leaving her best friend and supportive coworkers. But in the end, Ordoñez knew where she wanted to be. Excited and nervous on the first day of her new job, she told a superior—someone she knew and respected—that she was gay. She was hoping to find the level of comfort she'd left at GBLS. She was told that she should "keep it to herself," not the response she'd hoped for. Ordoñez gave him the benefit of the doubt; maybe he was looking out for her. Although it took about a year and a half, at some point, undaunted and not wanting to "watch pronouns," Ordoñez just began to tell people. She told one of the judge's clerks and asked her if she thought she could tell the judge; the clerk, clearly uncomfortable, had to admit that perhaps the judge already had heard about this. On another occasion, when Ordoñez approached one of the probation officers with an idea for training about legal issues for same-sex couples, "I have no idea why we need this" was the response.

When *Adoption of Tammy* was decided in 1993, it gave Ordoñez great pleasure to know that the very court she was a part of was recognizing the rights of the LGBT community. By 1995, Ordoñez was publicly out and not only serving on the MLGBA board, but also serving on the board of the Massachusetts Association of Hispanic Attorneys (MAHA). At MAHA's annual dinner one year, Ordoñez was scheduled to speak. A colleague introduced her and, among his other remarks, noted that she was on the MLGBA board. Even though she was more and more public about being a lesbian, she remembers having a moment of trepidation as she walked to the podium. No one missed a beat and she was relieved to realize it would not be a problem.

In 2000, Ordoñez applied to the bench. She was "hosted" by a professional on the South Shore (part of the nomination process is to have a host who shepherds you through the process). Before her interview with the Governor's Council, she told her host that she was going to introduce Carol at the interview. The host, in no uncertain terms, told her that he did not think this was a good idea and that "other councilors would have a hard time."

Ordoñez knew that she "would feel like Judas if I did not acknowledge our relationship." Carol thought perhaps they should just wait until her swearing in. Deeply troubled by the notion of not acknowledging "the love of my life" at such an important moment, Ordoñez asked advice of many friends and colleagues. She recalls that former Supreme Judicial Court Chief Justice Margaret A. Marshall told her, "Do what you think is right." Closer in time to the interview, Ordoñez once again asked her host whether he would still counsel her not to introduce Carol. She felt huge relief when he said, "Go ahead and introduce her, just don't dwell on it."

Carol's introduction did not derail Ordoñez's appointment to the bench, and when she was sworn in, she introduced Carol again as her partner. She and Carol married after the *Goodridge* decision and she admits it took a while to get used to introducing Carol as her "wife," but now it seems natural and fitting. Her marriage was never acknowledged by the person who told her she should "keep it to yourself." She proudly introduced Carol as the "love of her life," deserving of recognition for all her support, at a joint Boston Bar Association/Massachusetts LGBTQ Bar Association reception in her honor following her appointment as chief justice of the Probate and Family Court in 2013.

It took Ordoñez's own mother some time to get used to her being a lesbian. Her mother bore great shame about being an unwed mother. She wrote often to her own mother, back home in Colombia, but she did not share the news of her daughter's birth. Ordoñez's grandmother was illiterate and a neighbor would read the letters to her. It was just too shameful for her to think of the neighbor reading this to her mother. When the grandmother came to the United States for the first time when Ordoñez was three years old, they met, for the first time, when her grandmother walked through the airport gate. Fortunately, her mother's fears were ungrounded. Ordoñez and her grandmother bonded and her grandmother returned to the United States to help take care of her. Her grandmother learned to read a few years later and became a U.S. citizen at age ninety-two. Many years later, in her honor, Ordoñez legally took her grandmother's last name.

When she was appointed to the bench and the front page of her mother's local newspaper mentioned her involvement with MLGBA, her mother proudly announced to a neighbor, "That's my daughter. She has a female partner." And when she got married in June 2004, her mother told her, "This is the happiest day of my life because I never thought you'd get married. My daughters are equal now."

Ordoñez was appointed to the Nantucket Probate and Family Court, but spent the first three years as a circuit judge sitting in many courts before finding a home at Norfolk Probate and Family Court, where she felt the same comfort of acceptance as she had in her years at GBLS.

On November 16, 2003, Ordoñez called a recess shortly before 10:00 a.m. She went to her lobby, logged on to the Supreme Judicial Court website, and called Carol. She wept as she read the *Goodridge* decision aloud. Like many, it was hard for her to believe that marriage for same-sex couples would become possible in her lifetime.

When the U.S. Supreme Court announced its decision in *Windsor* on June 26, 2013, she was on the bench when an intern slipped her a note: "DOMA IS UNCONSTITUTIONAL." At that moment, she was overwhelmed with emotion again, realizing that the LGBT community had made incredible strides in a short period of time. She remarked, "It is so validating to have my marriage fully recognized at all levels of government and it is especially prideful knowing that the Massachusetts Supreme Judicial Court set this all in motion."

M. Barusch
Admitted 2009

As an undergraduate at Harvard Law School, M. Barusch (who prefers to be called "Barusch") was involved in the establishment of the Massachusetts Transgender Legal Advocates, a clinic designed to provide legal services to low-income and indigent transgender individuals. A group of law students, with the encouragement of the Massachusetts Transgender Political Coalition (MTPC) and only a couple of hundred dollars, began searching for a supervising attorney. Through an internship at AIDS Action Committee (AAC), Barusch became familiar with TransCEND (Transgender Care and Education Needs Diversity), an AAC program that provides support and risk reduction services to transgender women (male-to-female). Barusch recalls how challenging it was to find attorneys willing to help, until she discussed the idea with Attorney Denise Williams, then senior attorney at AAC, who volunteered to serve as the supervising attorney.

Founded in 2001, the MTPC is an organization dedicated to ending discrimination on the basis of gender identity and gender expression. Barusch sat on the MTPC steering committee during her law school years and served as vice chair for one year. She recalls with pleasure some small victories that resonate with the transgender community—the ability to change one's gender on a driver's license without the need for surgery, for example, which was negotiated directly with the Registry of Motor Vehicles.

MTPC was pivotal in obtaining the passage of "An Act Relative to Gender Identity" in November 2011, making Massachusetts the sixteenth state to add nondiscrimination laws for gender identity in the areas of employment, housing, K–12 public education, and credit. Massachusetts hate crimes laws were also updated to include gender identity.

Inspired by the Sylvia Rivera Project in New York City and motivated by the need to address the needs of low-income trans people, law students from Harvard University, Boston University, Boston College, Northeastern University, and Suffolk University became involved in MTLA. It took more than a year before MTLA could take on its first client in January 2008. The LGBT Bar Association and individual LGBT attorneys stepped up, as did several firms, to provide pro bono assistance. Wilmer Hale provided pro bono support in establishing MTLA's legal structure. Students working in the clinic soon discovered that their clients often had difficulty trying to accomplish the most basic goals, e.g., modifying or terminating a child support order or changing their names. More difficult issues were all that much more challenging. Clients reported being laughed at and scorned by court personnel ("Are you the mother or the father?"). What MTLA learned is that often the problem their clients faced was not so much obtaining the desired result from the court, but navigating the system to simply get before the court. MTLA advocates helped their clients navigate the system. MTLA was unable to sustain its activities and was forced to suspend its activities in the fall of 2012. It proved impossible to maintain the volunteer structure and ensure accountability and proper supervision. Barusch sadly reports that transgender litigants continue to face prejudice within the court system.

Barusch identified as transgender while in law school and reports that while she had generally positive experiences there, it was clear that Harvard wanted to be inclusive but did not always know how to do that. After graduating in 2009, Barusch obtained a clerkship at the Massachusetts Appeals Court, where she felt comfortable being out and where there were not only other out LGBT clerks, but also openly gay judges. After working for a short time in a small firm, Barusch found her legal passion at the Committee for Public Counsel Services (CPCS), which she describes as a "great place to be a queer person." At CPCS she found an environment where it is a priority to create an atmosphere nondiscrimination both for employees and for clients.

Surveys of the criminal justice system show that a disproportionate number of LGBT individuals have difficulty obtaining and keeping jobs, which of course translates to a disproportionate number of homeless LGBT individuals. Homelessness in turn is a precursor to involvement with the criminal justice system, because often these individuals have little or no family support. In fact, a large number of LGBT individuals in the criminal justice system also have previous involvement with the

Department of Children and Families. The Massachusetts LGBTQ Bar Association is currently working on a project addressing the legal needs of LGBT youth in the criminal justice system.

Barusch has seen slow, steady progress over the past few years with respect to transgender rights, but there is a long way to go. Training and education is needed from the ground up, from court personnel to lawyers and judges. Transgender individuals often face monumental obstacles in their ability, for example, to access beds in shelters, psychiatric, or drug and alcohol treatment. Although the passage of the transgender rights bill will certainly have an impact, until the law encompasses protection in public accommodations (which it does not), transgender people still have struggles to overcome.

When the bill was first introduced in the legislature, Barusch reports there was very little support. Things improved when the LGBTQ Bar Association and MassEquality (a statewide antidiscrimination advocacy organization) became more assertive about garnering support for the bill. It took three legislative sessions before the bill was finally passed. Ultimately, over 400 organizations (including almost all the minority bar associations, as well as the Massachusetts Bar Association and the Boston Bar Association), supported passage of the bill.

Like most LGBT lawyers, Barusch is a lawyer first, advocating for her clients, but she remains aware of the subtle ways discrimination shows up in her daily work. One benefit, though, that Barusch points out is that as a trans person who usually wears suits and ties, she's usually exempt from sexual harassment.

Changes in law have made it more possible for lawyers and judges to come out as LGBT. Even though issues still arise within the system, legal and cultural changes have had an enormous impact on the profession. Barusch points to a level of openness—for lawyers, judges, and litigants—that simply did not exist even five or ten years ago.

Special thanks to Gary Buseck, Esq., of GLAD, for his assistance on this chapter.

Timeline of Selected Notable Persons and Events

1978	Gay & Lesbian Advocates & Defenders (GLAD) is founded
1980	Fricke v. Lynch, 491 F. Supp. 381 (D.R.I.): GLAD successfully argues before the federal District Court that it was denial of a high school student's constitutional rights not to allow him to take a same-sex date to the junior prom.
1984	Boston Human Rights Commission is established to ensure full and equal access to public services and accommodations. The Commission enforces Boston's Human Rights Ordinance, which includes sexual orientation as a protected class. Openly gay attorney Frederick Mandel serves as the Commission's first executive director.
1985	Massachusetts Lesbian and Gay Bar Association (now the Massachusetts LGBTQ Bar Association) is founded.
1989	Dermot Meagher is the first openly gay man appointed to a Massachusetts court (Boston Municipal Court).
1989	The Gay Civil Rights Bill is passed by the Massachusetts legislature extending the protections of state antidiscrimination law to gays and lesbians in employment, housing, credit, and public accommodations.
1991	Linda E. Giles is the first openly lesbian women appointed to a Massachusetts court (Boston Municipal Court).
1993	Adoption of Tammy, 416 Mass. 205, allows adoption by unmarried individuals living together regardless of sexual orientation. Katharine Triantafillou is the lead attorney for the petitioners. A companion case, Adoption of Susan, 416 Mass. 1003, is led by Attorney Mary Bonauto.

1995	GLAD attorney John Ward is the first openly gay attorney to appear before and argue a case decided by the U.S. Supreme Court.7
1998	Bragdon v. Abbott, 524 U.S. 624, establishes that persons with HIV and AIDS are protected by the Americans with Disabilities Act. GLAD Attorney Bennett Klein is lead counsel.
2003	Goodridge v. Department of Public Health, 440 Mass. 309, allows same-sex couples to marry in Massachusetts.
2010	GLAD challenges the federal Defense of Marriage Act in Gill v. Office of Personnel Management, 699 F. Supp. 2d 374 (D. Mass.) and Attorney Maura Healey successfully leads the Attorney General's Office companion challenge in Massachusetts v. U.S. Department of Health & Human Services, 698 F. Supp. 2d 234 (D. Mass.). Both decisions are affirmed by Massachusetts v. U.S. Department of Health & Human Services, 682 F.3d 1 (1st Cir. 2012).
2011	An Act Relative to Gender Identity is passed by the Massachusetts legislature.

Endnotes

[1] GLAD has reported to MCLE that a Buffalo, New York, attorney named William Gardner may be the first openly gay man to appear before the U.S. Supreme Court. Gardner argued before the Supreme Court in *People v. Uplinger*, 467 U.S. 246 (1984), but the case was never decided as the Court dismissed the writ of certiorari as improvidently granted. The case involved New York's sexual solicitation law.

[2] Decisions on this subject included *Fort v. Fort*, 12 Mass. App. Ct. 411 (1981), and *Bezio v. Patenaude*, 381 Mass. 563 (1980).

[3] *Goodridge v. Mass. Dep't of Pub. Health*, 440 Mass. 309 (2003).

[4] 539 U.S. 558 (2003).

[5] 478 U.S. 186 (1986).

[6] 416 Mass. 205 (1993); 429 Mass. 824 (1999).

[7] See endnote 1, above.